To: <u>Rich & Roxanne France</u>

Please accept this book as a gift from the

two of us. It was written by our pastor,

Rev. Victor J. Grigsby of

Central Baptist Church. We hope it will bless

you as much as it has blessed us.

Sincerely,

Mel & Ti Anda Blount

Family Matters
Copyright © 2010 Victor J. Grigsby

Unless otherwise identified, Scripture quotations are from the King James Version of the Bible.

Penn Eagle Publishing
P.O. Box 6
New Brighton, Pennsylvania 15066

Printed in the United States of America

Lyrics used in chapter VI: *My Girl* , © 1964 by The Temptations, Gordy (Motown) Label. Lyrics in chapter X: *The Jesus in Me, Loves the Jesus in You,* © 2007 by Sam Tolbert. *I Love You,* by Lee Bernstein, Lyrics Publisher: © SHIMBARAH. *I Need You To Survive,* © 2002 by David Frazier, Verity Label

International Standard Book Number: 978-0-9828157-0-0

A Guide For Building Godly Homes

FAMILY MATTERS

VICTOR J. GRIGSBY

This book was written for my children:

Tareka – the Praised Humor   **Nekesha** – the Warm Affection

Nerissa – the Passionate Wonder   **Victor, II** – the Creative Strength

Alonna – the Crowned Queen   **Brian** – the Intellectual Observer

Clarissa – the Wonderful Gift

And dedicated first

to my beloved wife, Vickie, of twenty-six years who has been in my corner since the day we said, "I do" – and she still does!

And second, to:

"...all those who believe change is possible."

6

Acknowledgements

Thank you to all who take the time to read this material. I pray it will be a source of encouragement to everyone that comes in contact with its pages.

A special thanks to the Central staff and the Central Baptist Church for your prayers and for pushing me forward with this assignment – you are the best! My sincerest thanks and greatest appreciations are extended to the many wonderful friends that gave a listening ear to this book while it was yet a work in progress. Special thanks to Dr. Emma Lucas Darby, Chad Barnett, and Mel and Tianda Blount for your tremendous support and encouragement.

Thank you to my family for giving me permission to tell our story, for believing in me, and for your constant reminder that nothing is impossible – I couldn't have done it without you. Thank you to my wife and children for your patience during this creative time of my life.

And…Thank You God!…for giving me the words to write and the time to write it.

CONTENTS

INTRODUCTION

Family is a "learn-as-you-go" experience. Family is not something that can be figured out in a classroom, regenerated in a lab, or reproduced in a Boardroom. The formula for creating the functional family does not exist largely because no two families are exactly alike. Every family has its own characteristics, demeanor, and participants, which makes it difficult to ascertain a common prescription for how a family is to operate. We learn family as we live it.

However, in spite of the uniqueness that lies within each family, there are some common building blocks that can be used in any family to aid in developing a godly home. This book was written not to offer a formula for creating a functional family, but to establish practical guidelines and Biblical principles for building well maintained homes while using my own family as a guiding example of God's amazing power to transform.

Regardless of the frustrations, downfalls, struggles, trials and tribulations that every family experiences, family is the one place where everyone will have their entrance and from which everyone will make their exit –Family Matters!

Family keeps us grounded. Family keeps us stable. Family provides support. Family reproduces life. Family gives us structure. Family educates and establishes values. Family assigns roles and relationships. Family identifies destiny and determines direction. Family Matters!

Besides, I have always believed that change is possible, in spite of the difficulties a family faces, and that there is hope for struggling families to find new strength in God. Families that are beleaguered with maintaining a reasonable sense of solidarity and those who are distraught with finding meaningful and purposeful relationships are too numerous to mention. Family matters that are often overlooked are addressed here. Issues that rip at the heart of the family, problems that divide the home, troubles that try family values, and predicaments that throw family stability to the dogs are addressed in this body of work.

My mission in these few pages is to strengthen the family by offering Biblical insights to the roles and responsibilities of family members. I have not created an exhaustive commentary on family dynamics, family therapy or family counseling, but I pray enough of the essential make-up of family is presented to offer a reasonable hope to families everywhere. This is not a clinical manual or a psychological journal on family; it is my Biblical interpretation and personal testimony of what God can do with a family in the grips of dysfunction.

I am not the righteous guide for family – our Savior IS that – but God has entrusted me to direct families by exploring "family matters" with righteous instruction. How honored I am to present such words of hope and deliverance to families in crisis and to present proven tools of inspiration for families looking for ways to create a better home-life.

As honored as I am to receive such a mission, I am also tremendously intimidated to think that God has placed the care of family in my hands. I did not choose to write the book; I was given this work as a divine assignment to reach families for God.

The content presented here is a mixture of personal testimony, Biblical reference, spiritual principle, and practical living. With a unique blend of the sacred and the secular, I have attempted to present the family as a way of focusing again on the traditions that make family work. Inasmuch as this generation has become an anchorless people, no longer holding to the values and traditions that have solidified church and society for centuries, my aim is to reintroduce the fundamentals of a well-maintained and functional family. Family is held together by more than the cars we buy, the homes we live in, the vacations we take, and the degrees on the wall. The lasting bond within every home is the presence of God. This inspired writing defines the essential elements in building a godly home and the role of each of its family members.

While telling my own family story, I have traced my family from the edge of dysfunction to a family transformed and functioning in the Spirit of God. I share much of my family's story in hopes of offering one family's testimony of how God can take the worst of us and extract the best from us. Often presented with a spray of humor, I have presented the tensions, the conflicts, and the pains that would have left my family lifeless and loathsome except for the grace of God.

At times, the content within these pages sounds like preaching and at times it reads like colorful comedy. Prayerfully, however, the message will not be missed by the entertaining retelling of my family drama. My only aim is to present real life, mixed with real drama, relying on the real power of God for change. I have no degree in social work, nor am I a Family Therapist. I only offer my life's experience and the nearly three decades of pastoral counseling as I have aided countless families in their quest for spiritual health and family wholeness. Be inspired, and know that if God has transformed my family from a dysfunctional mob to a family placed on divine assignment, God can do it for yours too.

Chapter I

"Good Night, John Boy"

"A happy family is but an earlier heaven."
– John Bowring

"Except the Lord build a house they labor in vain that build it." – Psalm
127:1

I grew up with Jay Jay, Lamont, Greg, Wally, "Meathead" and the
"Beave." They were a few of my favorite past-timers. They
didn't live on the block or in the small, upwardly mobile,
predominantly Anglo Saxon community of Sewickley,
Pennsylvania that sat along the Ohio River where I was raised.
They were part of the Television Situation Comedies[1] of the 70's
that my family tuned in to as a part of our home's "educational"
programming. We watched *Good Times* with James and Jay Jay,
Sanford and Son with Fred and Lamont, *All In The Family* with
Archie and the "Meathead," and other favorites like *Leave It To
Beaver, The Brady Bunch,* and the beloved mountain drama with
John Boy from *The Waltons.*

My family ritualized *The Waltons'* reverberating "Good Night"
and would often call out to each other when silence had filled the
air and nighttime turned to bedtime.

"Good Night Jay."
"Good Night Junior."
"Good Night Elaine."
"Good Night Dad."

The refrains embraced the night until laughter overruled the
silence or until, more likely, our night calls became abhorred by our

father who would spoil our bedtime episode and tell us all to shut up and go to sleep because he had to get up to go to work in the morning. We watched these family oriented sitcoms not only to get our daily dose of wholesome family entertainment, but more importantly I watched these family "workshops" for the intellectual and educational moments and to learn how to deal with family issues. I needed to know how to absorb the punishment I received from my older brothers as they kept their little brother in line. I needed to know how to receive compliments without constraint from my sisters. I needed to know how to handle the discipline I received from my parents without internalizing it as hatred toward me. But what I needed most was to know my role as the youngest in the family, and how I could use my position as the "baby of the family" to my full advantage. I needed tactics to get the upper hand. I needed to understand the dynamics of the proper way to tattle, and how to use all the negative information I had collected on my brothers and sisters to my fullest benefit. Some of my skills I learned from "Jay Jay," some from "Greg" and "Peter," some from "*The Three Stooges*," and some I learned from the "Beave."

My family identified well with these sitcoms because in many ways we were the living version. We were the earliest untapped "family reality show"[2] of the time. We were not *The Brady Bunch*, or *The Waltons* on Waltons' Mountain, but we were a "bunch" nonetheless, and we did have a mountain of family mania. We had our "Meathead," "Big Dummy," and "Beave" too, but we called them "Rocket," "Mouse," "Boo," "Corkie," "Issy" and "Jay" (Walter, Doris, Elaine, Canard, Elizabeth and Victor). Three boys, three girls, a mom, a dad, a grandmother, and a dog named Major all resided in the same house.

We had more outrageous antics than a *Barnum and Bailey's Circus* on a Saturday afternoon with free give-a-ways – only too often I was the lion jumping through the hoop, the dog doing the tricks, the kid walking on the high wire, the boy eating the fire, and the sideshow for an extra dollar. We were often worse than the shenanigans at a *Three Stooges* convention.

Yet, we were a family and what we learned about home-life came from what aired on Saturday night, Thursday evening or any other program hour during the week. We didn't spend time in the Bible; the T.V. Guide was our Holy Book. Our family lessons came from its innocuous shows; although, my mother made us stop watching the *Three Stooges* because she said we had incorporated too many of their routines into our foolishness, and somebody was bound to get hurt.

Many families acquired their understanding of family and family roles the same way we did – from the television screen. Family guidance was a techni-color experience through an RCA tube on a twenty-seven inch screen. As a result of being overly engrossed with television, families looked to Edith and Archie Bunker, James and Florida Evans, and Mike and Carol Brady to find answers to their domestic problems. No wonder many families, including my own, struggled with dysfunction: unable to speak to one another, unable to appropriately resolve family conflict, unable to deal with family crisis, unable to work through the smallest of problems, unable to reach God because the solution for family problems and the instruction for family direction does not come through television sitcoms but from a Christ-centered, God oriented, home.

When families are struggling to stay together and facing crises, nothing is funny. It is no laughing matter when mothers and fathers are experiencing divorce. It is no laughing matter when a child is strung out on inhalants taken from the family cleaning supplies or when a child is hooked on heroine or crack cocaine. Nothing is funny when the sixteen year old daughter turns up pregnant, or the family is homeless because of a father's gambling addiction. Nothing is funny when alcohol becomes the answer to all of the family troubles and persistent abuse of wife and children are unleashed. Nobody is laughing when the refrigerator is empty and meat has to be stolen from the super market to put food on the table because the welfare supplement is not enough to feed the children. Nobody is laughing when a son becomes a victim of a drive-by and has his life snatched away before he has a chance to fulfill his dreams. Who is laughing when the children witness the continual physical confrontations of two parents who only know how to communicate with their fists? Who is laughing when a son is handcuffed and thrown in jail for selling drugs to sixth graders in the school playground? Tears replace laughter in the disheartening depths of dysfunction.

"Dysfunctional family"[3] has been the buzz word of the postmodern era to describe broken homes and its fractured

16

relationships. The phrase is so frequently used it is attached to every failing, unsuccessful, neglected, abandoned, and misguided situation in family life. I do not attempt to approach the subject of family dysfunction from a psychological description, but my aim is to evaluate family from its biblical and theological orientations.

A dysfunctional family is a family that lacks the ability to create the right domestic structure for producing proper values, morals, bonding, and responsibility among its members. Simply, dysfunctional family is a breakdown in relationship in the home and that breakdown occurs fundamentally because of a collapse in relationship with God.

> God is the foundation upon which all functional families are built.

Families that have become broken, fragmented, and torn, where family members haven't spoken to each other in years, where the presence of physical, emotional or sexual abuse is present, where violence is prevalent and the battered wife syndrome occurs, where the neglect of children and the fallout of addictions are rampant, we speak of them as a dysfunctional family. The dysfunctional family is the term used to address many of the haunting issues in families that tears them apart.

These chapters describe how God can take the dysfunctional family and transform it through His love and goodness into a family that is designed to fulfill the purpose and plan of God. This book identifies the power of God's amazing grace and goodness to redirect and restore family from its brokenness.

As I have witnessed in almost three full decades of ministry, every family is struggling with some dark and discouraging ordeal. Whether rich or poor, urban or rural, educated or uneducated, every family has some monstrous obstacle to overcome. The family continues to be at risk, and without God at the center, the family is destined for deterioration and disintegration. God is the foundation upon which all healthy families are built. "Except the Lord build an house they labor in vain that build it."(Psalm 127:1)

There is a wonderful parable that illustrates this point. It is the parable of the two men who built their houses on different foundations. The one built his house upon the rock, and the other built his house upon the sand. When the storms and the winds came and blew upon both houses, the man that built his house upon the rock, his house stood strong, but the one that built his house upon the sand, his house fell. And the Bible says "great was the fall of it."(Matthew 7:27)

The point is this: the rock upon which we build our homes is Jesus Christ. Anyone that will build his house on Jesus Christ, when adversity hits, troubles come, turbulence rises, and hard times approach will be able to endure. The goal of this book is to guide families in developing the proper foundation for building godly homes, and offers a description in understanding family roles. I want to probe the questions that every family ponders: What makes the family work? How does one build a happy and joyful home? What does the family that has God at its center, grace for its source, faith as its guide, truth as its standard, the Word as its strength, and heaven as its end need to do to stay together? By examining the roles of the husband and wife and their relationship with their children, answers will be gained. Not that I offer directed answers, but prayerfully what is presented is a standard and a format for deeper understanding of God's actions in the contemporary home.

What cannot be forgotten is that at the end of the day, after all of the ups and downs, after all the fights and family feuds, after all the personal indictments and individual accusations, after all the rumor mills have grinded family reputations into dust, when the lights are all out and silence has filled the air, and we, in Walton fashion, have bid each other good night, the only ones that will be there to embrace us, take us in, and offer us our best comforts and supports will be those who have walked with us, cried with us, laughed with us, and loved us unconditionally – our family.

18

Chapter II

Family Ties

"As the family goes, so goes the nation and so goes the whole world in which we live."

— Pope John Paul, II

"A house is built by wisdom, and it is established by understanding; by knowledge the rooms are filled with every precious and beautiful treasure."

— Proverbs 24:3-4

Fighting with my brother Canard every day had its lasting benefits. We didn't fight to kill; we fought to see who would ride the bike, get the last piece of raisin bread, or get to watch their channel on television. The immediate pain of it all was brutal as my arm was twisted behind my back, a punch was taken to my throat, a kick was landed in my chest, or a choke-hold was placed around my windpipe. These were loving matches that taught me how to negotiate with people on a much less physical level. It was not easy, but it was fun. It offered an understanding in human relationships that was invaluable and that would last beyond my adolescence.

Love and lunacy were both in our home with two brothers to fight, three sisters to pamper me, and a mother and father to keep me in line. I was the youngest, and I got my way – most of the time. I wined when I needed something, and when I needed attention I knew how to get that too.

20

I wasn't spoiled; I was loved. Spoiled is when something goes bad or sours and that I never did. I was loved, and it was the love of my family that kept me on the right path.

I was also blessed, but it took me years before I knew it. I never knew how blessed I was until I saw others who had much more than I, but appreciated what they had far less. I appreciated the squabbles with my brothers, the fights with my sisters, the punishments from my parents, and even the slobbers from my dog.

Dull moments in our home were extremely rare. At times I thought we suffered from some unnamed insanity, yet I knew its name – "Grigsby-itis." This family disorder was one that settled in the will and imbedded itself in the troubles of the mind. This family malady attacked our home's immune system and made us susceptible to every egotistical, self-centered, pride-driven phenomenon alive. Bitterness invaded us. Anger settled in. Internal competition ran rampant. External supports were nonexistent because we never sought to air our disputes in the community or discuss them with other families. We kept our issues to ourselves, so that "what happened in our home stayed in our home." What we would learn through all of the fussing and fighting was that God would set our family in order, and I would realize I was in the right place with the right people.

Unfortunately, haunting many of today's families are countless numbers of problems, setbacks, downfalls, and headaches that divide and destroy family ties. No day passes without some News report, article written, or joke made about families that are no longer productive or beneficial to its internal members or its external community. Every day we read or hear of families in crisis. Whether they have become victims to economic failure, violent crime, or personal abandonment, the family is under an incredible amount of pressure and facing a barrage of unbelievable problems.

Family instability is often a consequence of many of our own personal ineptitudes.

Family instability is often a consequence of many of our own personal ineptitudes. People can do such stupid things – especially those in our own family. Sometimes we sit back and shake our heads and wonder, "How could they be so stupid?" Yet, crazier things have happened to smarter, wiser, and richer people. Much of the trouble in our homes is blamed on our own lunacy, which is often true; however, neither can it be overlooked that the family is under attack by dark forces. Evil spirits and demonic influences are an underlying catalyst behind many of the misfortunes in our families. Believe it or not, Satan has always been out "to steal, to kill and destroy" (John 10:10), and the devil hasn't stopped yet.

The family is not excluded from satanic attack. The Devil wants to ruin, not raise, the family. Since the Edenic account of Adam's fall with the destruction of the family relationship between Adam and Eve, the Devil continually invades and interferes with our families only to destroy them.

Satan's aim is to cause a moral or emotional disconnect within the home and create a detachment from the divine purpose that God has for it. A family's purpose is rooted in an ancestral link within the family, so that if Satan can cause a disruption in the understanding of our past, he can disrupt the present family function. The problem with many families is that we don't know who we are, where we came from, or what we were intended to be. Part of that discovery comes from knowing our family history. We need to tap into our roots unless we are ripped from them.

The devil is still on his job. He is as active now as he was when he tempted Adam and Eve in the Garden of Eden. He is busier than ever trying to ruin our families and rip apart our homes. The devil wants to see the dismantling of family by starting as much aggravation, causing as much disturbance, and creating as much strife in the family as he can.

Family conflict is often camouflaged in "momma drama," and "family feuds."

Besides, what often looks like sibling rivalry, spousal conflict, childish rebellion, and parental dispute is really the family under demonic attack. Family conflict is often Satan camouflaged in "momma drama," "daddy deviance," and "family feuds." No family will agree on everything, but Satan knows how to use the disagreement to escalate it beyond its normal capacity into discord, and then accelerate the discord into family division.

The question is, "Why?" Why does the devil work so hard to destroy the family? Why does the devil work so diligently to cause such trouble in our homes? Why does the devil move so swiftly toward destruction in our relationships? The answer is *potential*. Every family on earth has the potential of becoming part of heaven's family, Lucifer's lost habitation.[1] Satan despises most the families of men becoming the family of God.

Everyday I see and talk to families that Satan is attempting to tear apart by whatever means necessary. The deceiver will use our children against us, husbands against wives, wives against daughters, sons against fathers. The devil will get in our finances, mess up our paychecks, disturb our lunch break, use our cell phones, flash images on our televisions, and even get in our pots and pans and turn the dining room table into a battleground of contention, strife and bitterness rather than a place of peace, blessedness, and togetherness.

Again, I don't mention the devil's invasion in our family crises as an excuse for weak morals, low values, or shallow minds. In times of family struggles and family obstacles, we cannot revert to and rely on the words of the voluptuous Flip Wilson character "Geraldine" and say, "The devil made me do it." The point here is to suggest that the family is under an all out attack whether by the unseen forces of evil or by the forces of our own human depravity.

Satan despises most the families of men becoming the family of God.

God wants the family back. Not that God ever lost it but that our Lord has designed family to live together by spiritual bonds, and to live out their God-given function. God is taking back the family. God is equipping the family for victory. No longer will God allow us to stand by and watch our families ripped apart by the devil, or our own moral collapse. One by one, home by home, household by household, block by block, and community by community, God is raising the family to meet its higher call.

God never meant for the family to be "dysfunctional." God has a specific function, a sacred assignment, for every family. When God created family in the Garden of Eden on the sixth day, scooped Adam out of the ground, and made Eve from his rib, and then said, "the two of you shall be one," God had a specific function in mind, primarily, to worship and glorify Him, and to occupy the place He had made. Man was to "dress and keep the garden." (Genesis 2:15) As the 19th century Pope Leo XIII explained, "the family was ordained of God that children might be trained up for Himself where father is prophet, priest and king and mother is highly honored and exalted, and children are the common bond of their care and love. It was before the church, or rather the first form of the church on earth."

Proverbs 24:3-4 reminds us that "a house is built by wisdom, and it is established by understanding; by knowledge the rooms are filled with every precious and beautiful treasure." It starts in the home.
What does?
Everything!

F	-	Father
A	-	And
M	-	Mother
I	-	Inseparably
L	-	Loving
Y	-	You

Everything starts in the home: our values, our manners, our religion, our time management, our work ethic, our behavior, our language, our conduct, our dreams, our hopes, our goals, and even our destiny. It all starts in the home. Part of the problem is that we have forfeited the role of the family in raising the next generation and given that responsibility to the schools, to the jails, to the government, and to the courts to raise our children.

God is tied to the family and within it the family is tied to its members. The **F.A.M.I.L.Y** is **F**ather **A**nd **M**other **I**nseparably **L**oving **Y**ou. God has tied the family inseparably together as His first ordained institution. Before there was the Church there was the Family. Before there was government there was family. Before there was law there was family. Before there was fraternity there was family. Before there was sorority there was family. Before there was University there was family. Before there was business there was family.

Any family that is not God-centered can be considered a dysfunctional family. For a family to be dysfunctional, it doesn't take a parent being violent toward their children or for one to be an addict, a gambler, or a drunk. Not putting God first in the home establishes grounds for dysfunction. Being self-indulged, me-centered, and self-directed makes a family dysfunctional. In fact, the Bible says in Proverbs 3:33, "The curse of the Lord is in the house of the wicked: but he blesses the home of the righteous." If God isn't in the home, how can it function properly?

There are problems and struggles in every family – yours and mine, Oprah's and Obama's, the churched and the unchurched, the saved and the unsaved. Every family has its drama – its baggage. However, the functional family is the one that knows how to support each other even when things are falling apart at the seams. The functional family is the one that gets knocked down but knows how to get back up with God. The functional family understands that everything doesn't go well all the time, yet through good times and bad times they know how to hang on to God. The functional family understands that even through the hazards of life, and the tribulations of living, the grace and the mercy of God will be the family's sustaining force. The functional family knows that no matter how bad the times the love of God is able to refresh, restore, and renew. Thomas Moore spoke of family crisis this way:

> Family is full of major and minor crises – the
> ups and downs of health, success and failure in
> career, marriage, and divorce – and all kinds of
> characters. It is tied to places and events and
> histories. With all of these felt details, life etches
> itself into memory and personality. It's difficult
> to imagine anything more nourishing to the soul.

Every family has someone that has fallen through the cracks, a "Black Sheep" of the family – a drunken Uncle Ned, a crazy cousin Butch, or a loose Aunt Matilda. As one unknown author mentioned, "Families are like fudge – mostly sweet with a few nuts." It is learning how to pray through the craziness in our homes that makes the family functional. It is calling on God through crisis that makes family a sanctuary for the soul.

In spite of all the madness, family is still our most enduring refuge. I am reminded of the words of Brad Henry: "Families are the compass that guide us. They are the inspiration to reach great heights, and our comfort when we occasionally falter."[2] At the end of the day, family is all we have, and family is where we turn for our personal comforts and endless joys. Family matters! When sick, we turn to family. When disappointed, we go to family. When kicked out, we seek family. When penniless, we call on family. When troubled, we run to family. To which, someone will open the door.

Again, as Pope Leo XIII said, "the family is the first form of the church on earth." There is a strong link between the dynamics in the home and the dynamics of the church. Families and churches are tied together. In fact, churches are made up of families, which suggest weak families mean weak churches, strong families mean strong churches, and dysfunctional families mean dysfunctional churches. We need to be reminded that the first church, the first ministry, the first prayer, the first song, the first worship, the first devotion is not the one we offer in Church on Sunday morning, but it is the one we create in the home during the week. Just as the church is our refuge and sanctuary from the world, so our homes are designed to be a place of peace on earth. Although often our greatest source of struggle, family can also be our greatest source of strength.

Just as the church is our refuge and sanctuary from the world, so our homes are designed to be a place of peace on earth.

Notice, God placed man in the Garden of Eden. He created the world in five days and then on the sixth day, God created man from the dust of the ground. God scooped out of the earth a chunk of clay and began to shape it, and form it, and mold it, and then after he had it just like he wanted it, he breathed into the nostrils. Divine CPR was performed, and the man became a living soul. He looked at the man and said for the first time after creating the world and all things therein, "It is *not good* for you to be alone," so he put the man named Adam to sleep, performed surgery on him, removed one of Adam's ribs and made from it a Woman. God called the man Adam and the man called the Woman Eve. They are the world's "First Family," and family is the first sacred institution ordained of God. Adam and Eve were created by God to take care of His creation, to populate the earth, and to have a relationship with their Creator.

This family tie is quite remarkable, or more accurately, quite sacred. God tied the family together. God gave life to Adam, Adam gave life to Eve, and Eve gave life to the world. In other words, the man gets his life from God, the woman gets her life from the man, and the world gets its life from the woman.

To understand these ties spiritually we glance at the theological force behind them. Jesus is represented in Adam, the

26

man. The church is represented in Eve, the woman. God gives life to the Son, the Son gives life to the Church, and the Church gives new life to the world. Ephesians 5:23-25 offers a biblical description of this spiritual structure:

> For the husband is the head of the wife, even as
> Christ is the head of the church: and he is the
> Savior of the body. Therefore as the church is
> subject unto Christ, so let the wives be to their
> own husbands in every thing. Husbands, love
> your wives, even as Christ also loved the church,
> and gave Himself for it…"

Regardless of what the family looks like, what it is going through, what the challenges are, family is of God. We cannot and should never forget that family is a *sacred institution*. The family is "Spirit-driven" and "Spirit-given." Family is God-made not man-made. God made family and all the sacred unions necessary within it. We don't put the family together, God does.

Isn't it interesting that none of us got to choose who our mother would be? Isn't it interesting that we didn't get to choose who our father would be? Isn't it interesting that we didn't get to choose our brothers and sisters? Family is predetermined before we arrive on the planet. Those are God's choices. God has placed us in the family of His choice. That's why it bothers me to hear brothers or sisters, daughters and sons say, "I hate you" to people in their own family. When we say we despise our brother, we are really saying God didn't know what He was doing. God knew exactly what He was doing. We are in the right place with the right people – and we don't get to complain!

Notice that in the functional family not only does God get to choose but He also sets the order. It was the Man first then the woman, then the children. The functional family recognizes the divine order in which God placed within it. The family becomes dysfunctional when the order is disturbed, when we've got men who want to be in the woman's place and women that want to take the man's place, and children that want to take the place of the parents. It won't work! I am not suggesting in a chauvinistic voice women "stay in their place," or children stay in theirs. What I am suggesting is that life follows a direction, an order. Man gives the seed to the woman, and the woman gives life to the world, and those fundamental contributions cannot be changed for life to occur. Reversing the "life-order" does not, and cannot produce anything.

God is a god of order. In the beginning, God created order (cosmos) out of chaos. And not only is order essential to the functioning of the world – every planet in its orbit, every particle on its plane, every person in their space – but order also undergirds the family and the church.

Adam was made first. Adam carries the first order or first responsibility in the family. Adam was made first to suggest that he is the head of the family, which is not to suggest that Eve is any less than Adam, yet it is clear from the order that God made man first for a reason. God could have made the woman first, but it would have defied the role and responsibility of the Second Adam, Jesus Christ, which was to come.

Even Adam's act of naming his wife reinforces his love for and leadership of Eve. Of course, Adam names the woman to identify with her, to communicate with her, and to honor her. But more importantly, the naming of the woman personalizes his relationship with her. God named Adam in order to be personal with him. Adam named Eve to be personal with her. We "name" and use names, whether it be for our cars, our animals, or with people because we want to be personal with them. As we are the "namer" and not the "named" we demonstrate that we are the holder, the leader, the possessor of the "object" named.

Notice Eve did not name the man because the man was to take the lead in love and personal relationship with the woman. That is not to be sexist but to stress a theological and spiritual principle of the church. Primarily, God named Adam and Adam named Eve to procure the relationship between them. It had to be that way because Adam represents Christ, and Eve represents the church. Christ came before the church and is the head of it, so Adam came before Eve and is the head of the woman. The life of the church came out of Jesus, and the life of the world is birthed from the church. In other words, Christ initiates the personal relationship he has with the world and expresses his love to it. We did not seek him; he sought us. We did not go to him; he came to us. Before we loved him, he loved us. God initiates the loving, personal, relationship we have with Him.

Furthermore, God saved his best creation for last. After he had made all the suns, moons, stars, the galaxies, the planets, the waters,

28

the vegetation upon the planet, the fish in the sea, and the animals upon the land God made man. He made man to be his pinnacle creation, His crowning glory. He saved the best for last – Man. Yet, after Adam came Eve. So that if God saved man for the best of his creation and Adam is the Glory of God, then the woman, Eve, is the glory of the man. She is literally the love of his life, the object of his affection.

It is love that people need that makes them feel connected in the world. Hate divides but love unites. People need to feel connected by love with someone. Every person in the family, to be whole and functional, needs to know there is love extended to them and that there is a support system they can rely on. If there is no love connection in the home, a person will make a connection in the street with gangs, other organizations or even another family. A sense of belonging is needed for every person's social, emotional, and spiritual development. The reference goes back to God saying, "It is not good for man to be alone."

Connection from person to person is necessary, so that as we lovingly connect with each other we might also connect with God. Relationship with others helps us to understand within us the capacity to love. As God is love, we connect to him by connecting to those around us. A profound verse of scripture speaks to this truth.

> Beloved, let us love one another: for love is of God;
> and every one that loveth is born of God, and knoweth
> God. He that loveth not knoweth not God; for God is
> love...If a man say, I love God, and hateth his brother,
> he is a liar: for he that loveth not his brother whom he
> hath seen, how can he love God whom he hath not seen.
> And this commandment have we from him, that he who
> loveth God love his brother also." (I John 4:7-8, 20)

That's Trinity: Father, Son, and Holy Ghost are God's capacity to love. God is a "relational" God. God must interact with someone and before there was anything to interact with the Father - the Lover, was loving the Son - the Beloved, through the love of the Holy Spirit, the Love.[3] God was in relationship with Himself. Ultimately, God created a world and families within it as love's expansion plan: "For God so loved the world that He gave His only begotten Son that whosoever believeth in Him should not perish but have everlasting life."(John 3:16)

That's Family: It stays together and is strengthened through its loving connections of father loving mother, mother loving daughter, father loving son, parents loving children, and children loving parents.

31

Chapter III

Handling Family Crisis

"The family is a haven in a heartless world."
— Christopher Lasch

"Now Jesus loved Mary, and her sister, and Lazarus."
— John 11:5

Perfect families don't exist. No matter how hard we try to make them so, or how much we believe they are, no family is without faults, mistakes, blemishes, or blunders that can erode the family structure. Families do their best to create the perfect home, a kind of Rockwell portrait, but unfortunately things happen that waste away the family formation, and tarnish our shining Rockwell image. Troubles, crises, and trials invade every family.

Exemptions to family perils do not occur. My family was not excluded from the things that could go wrong in a home. In fact, if it could go wrong, it did go wrong. I fought with my brother over any and everything. My brother scuffled with my sister for control. My mother clashed with my father in or out of bed. And my father grappled with us all. In between the brawls, like prize fighters in training, we would cool off, grow stronger in our relationships with each other, and determine new strategies of conflict resolution.

My earliest training was not just on the Little League baseball field, the Mighty Might football team, or in Karate class at the Sewickley Community Center, but some of my most effective preparation took place at home, with a beer, a bottle and a number. No one in the family had an addiction to drugs or alcohol (that I knew of); although, I was given my first *Millers* at age ten and my first shot of *Old Grand Dad* at age eleven. Although no one in the family had a gambling problem, I played my first number at age nine.

My Dad had a hot tip on a hot number – "713". We gathered our money. I broke my bank and handed my father ten dollars. Canard said we were crazy for wasting our money, but we didn't care what he said because we were about to be rich, and he would be begging us for money. My Dad ran down to *Smitty's Bar* to meet the man to play our number. We waited until after five o'clock because in those days the close of the Stock Market determined the number – needless to say my brother was right.

Abused I was not. Confused I was. I was not sure in my youthful years if we would remain a family. I was not sure if my parents would divorce. The breakup was inevitable the way they argued and considering how my father ruled his castle. For all I knew their marriage was on the rocks, and it was about to crumble fast.

My concern was if they divorced, where would we go? Who would I be with? Where would I sleep? Who would take care of me? I hoped the severity of my anxiety was more my imagination than actual fact, yet I saw too often my mother unhappy, and heard her say too frequently she would leave that man…"If." I never knew upon what conditions she would make her exit, at what point the time would be right, or when she would have had enough. "If"— she didn't have so many kids? "If" – she had more income? "If" – she had some place to go? "If" – she didn't have so many years already invested in their relationship? "If" – she had gotten her High School diploma or G.E.D.? "If" – she was not afraid to go it alone? "If" – she didn't love him so much?

Although I had my ungrounded suspicions about what was causing the family feud, I never really knew why my mother felt that way, or what caused her to stand at the kitchen sink and stare out the window into clouds of despair. She was troubled but had no one to turn to and few friends to rely on.

When they would argue at night, I would curl up under my covers, and tuck my head under the sheets and listen to my father's rage. Would he hit her? Would he throw something at her? If he did, I would be the one to defend her. But who was I kidding? What could a nine year old do? The best I could do was hope for a quicker morning, so that I could get up and go to school. Yet, the nights often seemed to last forever and the rage was intensified by the chilling darkness.

I didn't know then, but our family was not unlike those described in the Bible. The biblical families were also saturated with drama and confusion, yet there they were eternally etched in the Holy Scripture. They were families in crisis, and they were presented in God's Word. These troubled biblical families remind us that our families are no different from our own – no family is exempt from turmoil and strife.

In the beginning with the first family of Adam and Eve and the tragedy of their son Cain killing his brother Abel, every family since then has had its chaos and deadly drama. Noah's family, in Genesis chapter nine, experienced extreme embarrassment due to Noah's drunkenness. Abraham's family, in Genesis chapter sixteen, was in turmoil because Abraham tried to short circuit the promise of God by having a baby by another woman. Eli's family, in I Samuel chapter four, experienced crisis with his two sons Hophni and Phinehas, two boys out of control that desecrated the temple. And King David's family, in II Samuel chapter thirteen, experienced total bedlam when David's son Amnon raped his sister Tamar.

These families, along with many other biblical examples, demonstrate for us there is not, never as been, nor ever will be a family that does not have some crisis to confront, some issue to resolve, and some madness to deal with.

In this chapter I offer an appraisal of a New Testament family that lived in Bethany, a little town that was located on the east side of the Mount of Olives less than two miles east of Jerusalem. They were an average family dealing with average issues. They were not rich by any means and barely had enough resources to make it like most of us. They had to deal with putting food on the table, and sister to sister tensions, and brother to sister squabbles just like all of us. At times they would invite folk over, but they had no extraordinary setting, no red carpet displays, no fancy feasts, or fabulous placements. This family was average and average at best. They were two sisters Mary and Martha and their brother Lazarus.

Martha was more likely the oldest since she had a way of taking the lead in most of their affairs. She was always the one planning the dinner and making sure everybody was comfortable, and everybody had enough to eat, and everything was tasty. She was a bit impatient and overly concerned herself with mundane matters. Mary, on the other hand, had great spiritual desire and discernment and was willing to sacrifice her most precious commodities for Christ's sake. And Lazarus just sat back and took it all in not bothering anybody, and certainly not getting in their way.

The family consisted of three adults living together in one household, three grown people sharing the same home, three grown folk living together. They were three individuals trying to make it through life the best they could. Why they never established homes of their own we are not told. Why they were still living together and not married, we do not know. Maybe it was because no man could put up with Martha's sassiness. Maybe it was because Mary wanted to be in church all the time. Maybe it was because Lazarus was too much a homebody and no woman wanted to have to go through his sisters to get to him. Obviously though, with all they had to deal with there was a lot of love between them evidenced by the mere fact that they were living together.

In fact, their family looks a lot like our own – trying to make it the best we can – struggling with money problems, paying bills, keeping food on the table, the lights on and the water running. These were *Good Times:* "Keeping your head above water, making a wave when you can. Temporary layoffs…Easy credit rip offs…Scratching and surviving…Good Times."[1] They were living paycheck to paycheck and one check away from the soup line.

This Bethany family was much like ours hoping for the best but often experiencing the worst. Their family looks much like ours hoping that a Bail-out would come past Wall Street and touch Main Street, and one day come down "My Street." This Bethany family is much like ours, sometimes fighting, other times fussing, but together nonetheless.

This Bethany family was maintaining a decent quality of living until one day Lazarus got sick. Perhaps his illness resembled a common cold at first, but it progressed into something much worse. It became more than they could handle.

This family of Mary, Martha, and their brother Lazarus is now in crisis as uncontrollable, unexplainable, and unpredictable things happen in every family. There is no real godly explanation to it. It just happened. No real theological reason behind it. The crisis just came. There is nobody to which to point the finger. It is just a painful predicament that planted itself in plain people. Nobody is at fault. No one is to blame for the misfortune. Sometimes things just get out of control and life takes a turn for the worse. Layoffs come. The baby arrives. The drought comes. The car breaks down. The hurricane comes. The children fight. The wife acts up. The husband goes off. It happens today and sometimes tomorrow, but trauma and calamity does show up.

Lazarus' sickness escalated and now their brother was dead. A cold had turned into a crisis. And the question becomes what does the family do when crisis hits? How do you handle the mishaps, misfortunes, and maladies of life as a family in Crisis? Especially in tough economic times, with gangs in our streets, with violence everywhere, with communities building casinos to stimulate economic growth, with inner city education at an all-time drop out rate, with single parent mothers as heads of households higher than ever, what do we do?

The answer lies in the response of Mary and Martha when their brother Lazarus died. In fact, the crisis was so bad for Mary and Martha that not only was Lazarus sick, and not only did his sickness turn to death, but now their crisis was "stinking." Death had escalated to decay. Although the situation was tucked away in a tomb, their family crisis had started to smell and everybody in town knew it was stinking.

Family crises can bring death to relationships, but more critically crises can also decay the values and beliefs that create the family bond. When the moral and spiritual fiber of a family begins to decay, everyone can smell it. Even though we try to cover it, hide it, or camouflage it, the stench of decaying family is obvious. At the backyard cookout someone says, "You smell that?", and they aren't talking about the chicken barbecuing on the grill. At the Thanksgiving Day dinner there is an odor in the air and everybody knows it is not the turkey or the yams that's got the house smelling. Nobody's talking about anything because they've got it tucked away in a cave with a stone rolled in front of it, but the smell is still in the air.

> **Even though we try to cover it, hide it, or camouflage it, the stench of decaying family is obvious.**

Mary and Martha's crisis was stinking, yet what can't be overlooked is that this family was also loved by Jesus. The key to crisis intervention is in verse five where it mentions, "Jesus loved Martha, and her sister, and Lazarus." Not just anybody was in crisis, but the ones that were loved by Jesus were in crisis. What can't be overlooked is that because Jesus loves us all, Jesus is able to take any family in crisis and bring any dead situation back to life. The power of God in Christ Jesus can restore, revive, and renew any family situation to its appropriate godly status. Dead marriages, dead relationships, dead dreams, dead finances, dead ambitions, dead opportunities, dead communications, dead businesses, dead homes can all come back to life.

In fact, there is a move of God upon all families such that whatever has gotten the family down, whatever has died in the family, God is going to resurrect it and restore it. The story of the raising of Lazarus is a restoration text. It is about "Come Back!" It is about Getting Up! It is about Resurrection! And today is the day to look at the dead places in our families and call them forth to new life.

One element in the restoration of family is essential – *acknowledgement*. Acknowledgement of any bad situation is critical to family survival. In order for family to be restored, acknowledgement of the situation has to be engaged first. Acting like nothing is wrong is sterile. Denial is not an option. Mary and Martha assessed the situation accurately. They did not deny their problem. They did not deny they had a crisis. They called it what it was. They knew it. Everybody knew it. The entire town knew this Bethany family was operating on code red. When families start sweeping troubles under the rug, problems turn into crises. Recognize the situation for what it is.

Once the situation is acknowledged and accepted for what it is then we are wise to do what Martha did – Call on Jesus – Pray! When crisis hits, and the situation is stinking, and death is everywhere, and there is no place else to turn – call for Jesus. The sisters sent for Jesus on behalf of their brother. Too often families break down during their crisis instead of a breaking through because they call on the wrong person. They call on the wrong name. To call on the name of government, the name of universities, the name of Wall Street, Hollywood or Huntington is only a limited help at best. Even calling on friends and family is an inadequate response for the real spiritual restoration that is needed.

The only right response in crisis is a faith response – a calling on the name of the Lord. Faith is critical for restoration. Martha said, "Lord, if thou hadst been here my brother had not died, But I know, that *even now*, whatsoever thou wilt ask of God, God will give it thee." Her brother was dead, but she still had faith enough to believe that Jesus could handle the situation – *even now*. In every family crisis, *"even now"* faith is essential to restoration and renewal. When the family situation is beyond hope, an "even now" faith is needed to get the home back in righteous order. "Even now" I can get my husband back. "Even now" I can have my relationship with my wife restored. "Even now" I can be financially restored. "Even now" my home can be a loving place. Your faith will keep you going. Your faith will see you through. Your faith will sustain you.

Jesus says to Martha, "Thy brother shall rise again." And Martha says, "I know that he shall rise again in the resurrection at the last day." Then Jesus responds by saying, in verse 25, "I am the resurrection and the life: he that believeth in me though he were dead, yet shall he live." This is the restorative statement in family crisis because when a family is in crisis they have to recognize who Jesus is. If the family is going to come back from crisis, the family will need to understand that Jesus *IS* the resurrection and the life – right now! Not will be, not was, but IS for the present dying situation the resurrection and the life for the family.

After all, who do we think Jesus is? He is not some wimp sitting on the side of the universe holding on for dear life. He created this world. He is the Lord God Almighty. "Thou art worthy to receive glory and honor and power: for thou hast created all things, and for thy pleasure they are and were created."(Revelation 4:11) God does not find pleasure in human suffering.[2] God does not find pleasure in family crisis. If he did, he would be a sick god. He would be a sadistic god, a god that gets his kicks through human suffer. That is not the God we serve. He is the resurrection and the life for any of life's challenges and the family's difficulties.

Martha then went her way, and called Mary her sister saying, "The Master is come, and calleth for thee." Mary gets to Jesus and says, "Lord, if thou hadst been here my brother had not died." Then, when Jesus saw her weeping, and the Jews also weeping, he groaned and was troubled, and said "Where have you laid him?" They pointed out the place of pain. They identified the place of sorrow, and acknowledged the place of death. In recovering from any crisis point, the family has to identify the place of pain. The "crisis place" has to be pointed out. With no denial, no avoidance, no rejection or contradiction, the place of pain needs to be pointed out when families are in turmoil. Furthermore, too often families have been in crisis so long that we don't even know what is troubling us any longer.

They showed him where the dead place was in their family, and the Bible says, "Jesus wept." Jesus weeps because Jesus identifies with family crisis. Whatever the pain, we don't go through the struggle by ourselves, but Jesus goes through with us. David testified of the comfort of God and the presence of the Lord in times of crisis as he articulates it this way, "Yea, though I walk through the valley of the shadow of death, thou art with me."(Psalm 23:4) Families don't go through turmoil by themselves – God goes through with them. God identifies with our pain. He associates with our brokenness. He understands our human limitations.

Mary, Martha, Jesus and the others get to the place where Lazarus was and the Bible says, "It was a cave, and a stone lay upon it." Too often when we deal with family crisis what we want to do is bury that which is dead. We want to drop it in the ground, put it in a cave and get rid of it that we might go on with our lives. Then we put a stone in front of the situation to seal it, to say that's enough, to say it's over, to say finished. But to deal with family crisis the stone must be removed –"Take Away The Stone."(vs. 39)

The stone is identified as the thing that stops the family from being effective and productive, but the good news is that the stone does not and will not stop God. The stone represents Human Limitation. When faced with crisis what we do is roll stones in front of the dead thing because what we are saying is that there is nothing else we can do. But Jesus said to Mary "[I told you] if thou wouldest believe, thou shouldest see the glory of God." In other words, "man's extremities are still God's opportunities." We put the stone in front because of *our limitation*, but when the stone is rolled away it is done for *God's exaltation*. Possibility is paramount when the stone is moved away! Never forget that "with God all things are possible."

Jesus speaks to the family crisis and says, "Lazarus, Come forth." He calls Lazarus by name because if the family will be restored from the current crisis we have to "call it what it is." Name the crisis in your family. Call it what it is. Call it lying. Call it gambling. Call it alcoholism. Call it stealing. Call it murder. Call it envy. Call it pride. Call it hypocrisy. Call it revenge. Call it lust. Call it bitterness. Call it laziness. Call it anger. Call it strife. Call it whatever it is, but call it forth so that the Lord can speak to the crisis and restore it back to a place of prominence.

Jesus looks at Mary and Martha and says I give your brother back to you. I restore your family to you. By the power of the Lord Jesus Christ, Lazarus came forth from the tomb standing tall.

The good news is that as Jesus Christ restored Mary's family, by the same divine power He can restore any family. He can say to any family facing crisis, I give your brother who was dead in the streets back to you. I give your sister who was dead on crack back to you. I give your mother who was dead to gambling back to you. I give your father who was dead to incarceration back to you. I give your son who was dead in fornication and pornography back to you. I give your daughter who was dead in pride and conceit back to you. I give your family who was dead in shame, and dishonor, and disgrace back to you. There is no family that God cannot take from the deepest levels of despair to a renewed place of holiness, righteousness, and goodness in Him. No matter how decayed the family, God has the ability to restore it and raise it to new life.

Chapter IV

A Job To Do

"A man travels the world over in search of what he needs, and returns home to find it."

      – George Moore

"In the sweat of thy face shalt thou eat bread, till thou return unto the ground; for out of it wast thou taken: for dust thou art, and unto dust shalt thou return."

      – Genesis 3:19

When my Dad said, "Let's go!"…we went. With no questions asked and no rebuttal given, we climbed in the back of his green Dodge pick-up with our lips dragging the ground and went off to carry our next load. We were "Grigsby and Sons." We knew it; our friends knew it, and everybody in town knew that *Sanford and Son* had nothing on us. We could pick up junk, move trash, and haul furniture with the best of them. My Dad didn't care what we were doing when he said, "Let's go!" We were always on call. Playing basketball at the Elementary school playground, riding bikes on Centennial Avenue, or swimming at the Community Center pool was often interrupted by a toot of the horn and a summons with his finger. We were called to duty. We had to ride in the back of the truck and hang on to all the junk we had loaded. Whether it was a load of bad appliances we were taking to the salvage yard, a load of aluminum siding we picked up from somebody's remodeling job, a load of furniture we were moving for a neighbor, or piles of shrubbery and hedge clippings cut from one of the local's yards, we would ride to the dump hoping that one trip for that day was enough.

Occasionally, a fight would break out in the back of the truck or in somebody's yard between my brother and me. Because I didn't get the rake or because he was trying to be my boss, we would light into each other like two Rhode Island Reds in a cock fight. My Dad would whip us back into shape and remind us that we had a job to do, and we could kill each other later.

Our job was to do what he told us. We were the hired hands but never seemed to get any compensation for our time. We never got a raise because we never got paid. My father said the pay was good – "You eatin' and sleepin' ain't you?"

Although we very rarely got any money for our labor, what we did receive was priceless. We got a work ethic that would carry us through life. We learned that hard work does pay off, such that, according to my father, "If you want something in life, you've got to work for it." We received the undeniable satisfaction of knowing that we contributed to keeping Duquesne Light satisfied and Columbia Gas from calling. More importantly, however, we learned the essential elements that make family function.

From the back of a rusty pick up truck I learned a great deal about emotional stability, physical health, psychological well-being, and the indispensable building blocks that a family needs to possess for it to function properly. As Dr. Tina B. Tessina, Psychotherapist, self-help author, and licensed Marriage and Family Therapist, mentions in her book: *It Ends With You: Grow Up and Out of Dysfunction*, "A healthy family should create and sustain an environment which promotes emotional and physical health and psychological well-being for its members."[1]

Before I list the essential family building blocks and their brief descriptions, I begin with one obvious family focal point: a functional family must be a *Praying* Family! Of all the building blocks to be mentioned, none of them have the lasting impact of one prayer. Prayer is the family anchor. Prayer is the family fastener. Prayer is the clasp to which all other family activity is affixed. Besides as once said, "the family that prays together stays together."

Thomas Louis Haines mentioned in 1882 that "a prayerless family cannot be otherwise than irreligious…" Truer words

concerning the family could not have been written. What
else connects a family to God and to each other but prayer? He
went on to write:

> What scene can be more lovely on earth, more like
> the heavenly home, and more pleasing to God, than
> that of a pious family kneeling with one accord around
> the home-altar, and uniting their supplications to their
> Father in heaven! How sublime the act of those parents
> who thus pray for the blessing of God upon their
> household! How lovely the scene of a pious mother
> gathering her little ones around her at the bedside, and
> teaching them the privilege of prayer! And what a
> safeguard is this devotion, against all the machinations
> of Satan!

> It is this which makes home a type of heaven, the
> dwelling place of God. The family altar is heaven's
> threshold. And happy are those children who at that altar
> have been consecrated by a father's blessing, baptised by
> a mother's tears, and borne up to heaven upon their joint
> petitions, as a voluntary thank-offering to God. The home
> that has honored God with an altar of devotion may well
> be called blessed.[2]

Ninety years after these words were written my grandmother
led us to the altar. She was the praying one in my family. Later we
learned the value of prayer and that through all of our internal
turmoil, hostility, ranker, profanity, and abuse it was prayer that
held our family together.

The building blocks of family are needful to list. A lengthy list
it is; however, these essential family qualities cannot be overlooked
if the family is to function properly.

Forgiveness. One of the most important building blocks of a
functional family is the ability to forgive. Forgiveness keeps a
family unified. No matter how well morally adapted and socially
secure a family may appear to be from the outside, every family has
its internal problems. Mistakes will be made in judgment, errors
will be made in relationship, and faults will occur that will create a
breach within the core structure of the family. To ignorantly think
that nothing ever goes wrong and no one ever does wrong within a
family is fanciful and delusional at best. Things happen! Bad
things happen in every family and every relationship so that

forgiveness becomes the safety net to which every miscalculation in judgment and misdirected deed falls.

Every family has faults, and everyone within the family makes mistakes. No family is perfect! Every family has its share of idiosyncrasies, ineptitudes, and flaws. If there is one thing that should be learned early in life, it is that we all make our fair share of mistakes. Margaret Laurence said, "In some families, *please* is described as the magic word. In our house, however, it was *sorry*." The one quality that keeps family coming back to each other is the willingness to forgive.

Forgiveness is necessary in every home because without it grudges build up and become uncrossable walls, bitterness clogs up the soul, and fifteen year walls remain stationary. "At the end of the day," according to Mark V. Olsen and Will Sheffer, "a loving family should find everything forgivable."

We learned as a family to make peace quickly, come back together openly, and not to look for faults because if faults are looked for, they are sure to be found. When a person has a forgiving heart, no score is kept on how many wrongs are done. The words of Jesus surely apply when he was asked, "How many times shall I forgive my brother?" and the Lord replied, "seventy times seven," (Matthew 18:22) or as many times as it takes.

Acceptance. Family is the one place where a person can be who they are without embarrassment or embellishment. Acceptance offers a boost in personal enrichment and is necessary for family operation. With family, there was no need to be pretentious in person, artificial in manner, or counterfeit in conduct. Being what we are and knowing that it's not what we do but who we are that counts. Genuine character is best policy. The critical commentary on Adam and Eve is that "They were both naked...and were not ashamed,"(Genesis 2:25) in other words, they were free to express their individuality without embarrassment or insult. In family, a person should be totally accepted without having to conform to world image, social pressure, or cultural limitations.

Motivation. Everyone in the family needs motivated to move to the next level of their personal enrichment. Most of the time a family member only needs pushed a little to reach their fullest potential. My motivation came on the back of my father's pick up truck. One of the greatest motivators in life is in knowing what you don't want to do for the rest of your life. I knew early that I did not want to haul rubbish all my life, not that hauling rubbish on a truck was not a worthwhile and respectable job, it was just not for me. It was too hard. I wanted to work smarter not harder. I would rather work with my head than with my hands. School, a degree, and corporate America became my goal.

Instruction. If my father taught us nothing else, he taught us how to follow directions and how to, from those directions, develop a strong work ethic. He showed us the value of a hard day's work. He showed us that following directions were important. He taught us how to work. Leave the rake in the yard, when he told you to pick it up, could cost you another day's free labor. He taught us what it meant for a man to "eat by the sweat of his brow" and how to be proud of it.

Love. From all of the trash hauling, furniture moving, hedge clipping, and grass cutting, we learned that it takes a genuine care, concern, and affection for one another to get the job done. We worked because we cared, and we cared because we loved. We cared what happened to our brothers and sisters. We didn't realize then, but years later we

> Love makes you feel good about yourself and about those around you.

understood that the compelling force behind our constant corner pick-ups was the power of love.

Money doesn't make a family. Neither does a fancy car, a backyard swimming pool, or a Disney World vacation. Love creates the bonding within a family and makes home the place a person can always come back to after countless bitter encounters with the world. I agree with Robert Hugh Benson, "The union of family lies in love; and love is the only reconciliation of authority and liberty." Bernie Wiebe also mentioned "Loving relationships are a family's best protection against the challenges of the world." Love makes you feel strong, important, and appreciated. Love makes you feel good about yourself and about those around you.

You. In this first grouping of essential family qualities, the last to be mentioned is You. Family is where individuality is complimented not criticized. If in no other place, the family allows a person to be who they are without inhibitions, restrictions or reservations. In the family, you are who you

> In the home, a person is celebrated for their personal uniqueness and style.

are and can be what you want to be. Family is the only real place where a person is free to be who they are. In the home, a person is celebrated for their personal uniqueness and style. In family, you are valued, you are important, you are irreplaceable. Think of it, if you were removed from the family, your family would no longer be what it is.

I agree with the words of Virginia Satir that "Feelings of worth can flourish only in an atmosphere where individual differences are appreciated, mistakes are tolerated, communication is open, and rules are flexible -- the kind of atmosphere that is found in a nurturing family."

Finally, I introduce some additional building blocks that will be the basic constructs for the functional family.

Faith. A family cannot function properly without faith – faith in each other, faith in oneself, and most importantly faith in God. When nobody else believes in you, family demonstrates a confidence in you that is uncompromised. Jim Valvano once said, "My father gave me the greatest gift anyone could give another person, he believed in me."

Understanding. A family must also be understanding. Every member of the family must have the ability to put oneself in the other's place to avoid criticism or condemnation. Each member must be true to a fault but not as becoming an enabler for errant and destructive behavior.

To understand is to show respect. It is not something to be earned but to be extended as a personal dignity. When each family member understands another's need for space, values another's opinions, accepts their need for privacy and need to be heard, respect is gained. Understanding and respect create proper boundaries that are set and maintained within the home. Parents remain parents and children remain children without an overlapping or overindulging in the familial roles.

Nurturing. Every family member needs nurtured. The proper mental, physical, and emotional nourishment is needed for each member of the family. Malnourished families become dependent upon other self-satisfying and often self-destructive substances.

Communication. Families often become dysfunctional because of communication problems. Either every one is talking and no one is listening, or no one is talking at all. Too often the members within the family talk *at* each other rather than *with* each other. Everyone talking with no one listening is not communication; that is collective noise. Communication is listening with earnest. It is the ability to speak from and hear with the heart.

Trust. Families are networks of trust. Dysfunctional families are those families that live with constant skepticism, doubt and unbelief towards one another. There are more questions asked than kindnesses given. One thing functional families do well is trust each other. Where trust is unbiased confidence, every family member receives affirmation without personal indictment. Without trust family relationships are always on edge, looking over their shoulder, and unable engage each other with honesty and openness.

> Families are networks of trust.

Involvement. Every person in the family is a legitimate participant in the family's overall success. Everyone has a significant role because everyone in the family has something to offer.

Good families are created because everyone in the family is willing to get involved, do their share, and contribute where needed. Collective effort from each family member is essential to family stability because each member needs to feel they offer a significant contribution to the overall family. When one of the members of the family is left out of the family as a work group, a productive unit, there is a lack of individual necessity – the family is basically saying, "We don't need you." When everyone gets involved in sustaining the home-life, each member is valued and feels appreciated. A family works best when everyone in it participates toward the family's greater good.

Opportunity. Creating opportunity for each member of the family to grow is essential to proper family function. No member of the family should be denied the opportunity to display their gifts, talents, and skills. In fact, opportunity should not just be "given" but made for each family member to showcase their abilities.

Nobility. Maintaining dignity within the family is the crowning enterprise for every family. Each member of the family should hold the family in highest regard. Never let anyone talk about your family. My family was taught to take pride in our family and in our home. We were "Grigsby's," and we were reminded to be proud of it. We were told that there were certain things that "Grigsby's" didn't do. We were told that "Grigsby's" were not better than anybody else but that we weren't worse than anyone else either.

F	- Forgiveness		**F**	- Faith
A	- Acceptance		**U**	- Understanding
M	- Motivation		**N**	- Nurturing
I	- Instruction		**C**	- Communication
L	- Loves		**T**	- Trust
Y	- You		**I**	- Involvement
			O	- Opportunity
			N	- Nobility

These are the essential building blocks of a functional family, and what cannot be overlooked in the functional family is the FUN in *Fun*ction. Families falter because they forget to have fun together. God made family to be enjoyed and for the members of it to enjoy each other – have a good time together. A functional family learns to enjoy each other's company.

When family becomes boring and dull, and tedium sets in, family soon breaks down because the appreciation and excitement for each other has diminished. When new life is birthed into the world and the family expands with a bouncing and bubbly baby boy or girl, excitement fills the home. Signs are posted: "It's a Girl!" Cigars are passed out: "It's a Boy!" Somewhere in the daily pressures of family that excitement is lost. For a family to be functional that excitement must be regained.

Too many times I have sat across from families that have lost the elements of a happy home, and have replaced laughter with loathing, and encouragement with indictment. They sit across from each other but no words are exchanged only looks that could kill. They haven't walked through a park, thrown a Frisbee, or listened to the "Oldies" in years, or gotten involved in any bonding activity. Then they wonder why the gloom and doom in their home. For the

49

dysfunctional family, there is no fun; it is a constant battle
to stay under one roof together and maintain some appearance of
family structure. Home-life only possesses a spirit of boredom and
wall-to-wall monotony.

My family didn't need to look outside of our home for fun and
amusement; we had all we needed right at home. I didn't need to
find someone to play with; I had my brothers and sisters. We
laughed together about any and every thing – over a game of
Monopoly, while eating Coraopolis Pizzeria pizza, or while
watching The Flip Wilson or The Carol Burnett Show. We had fun
together without embarrassment because our motto was: "We crazy
– and we know it!" And through it all, we learned to laugh, love,
and live.

The qualities I have mentioned help sustain a functional family
and keeping the "fun" in function is without exception. Families
should teach the values and create the core orientations that support
its members and move them toward their higher order in God.
Every family, whether secular or Christian, can function; however,
what makes a family function with grace, operate in love, and move
in freedom is not just doing a job and doing it well, it is the ability
to operate in the Spirit of God and fulfill the family's deeper call.
Being moral and "good" is not enough. A functional family has a
mission to fulfill, a divine assignment to carry out for God.

50

Chapter V

Super Man

"Every man who is happy at home is a successful man, even if he has failed in everything else."
— William Lyon Phelps

"Blessed is the man that walketh not in the counsel of the ungodly, nor standeth in the way of sinners, nor sitteth in the seat of the scornful."
— Psalm 1:1

My father was the "man of the house." What that meant we were not sure considering my mother had just as much influence, direction, and control in our house as my father. He had a stronger, deeper, and louder voice than anyone in the house, but my mother was often the voice of authority, could make us move, and could get things done at about a three to one rate over my father. She could manage the money, shop for her children, and work a nine to five just like he did. Yet, he was the "man of the house." We knew it, and he made sure everybody in the house knew it.

He was a *GunSmoke* man. My father enjoyed Festus, Kitty, Doc, and the Marshall - Matt Dillan. In fact, he loved any Western show: *The Rifleman, Bonanza, The Virginian* – it didn't matter to him as long as he got to enjoy the Wild Wild West and see the open range, and the old guys in their cowboy hats sporting their spurs, and carrying their Winchesters.

We once took a trip to Kansas. My father said we were going to see my mother's brother, Uncle Junior, and Uncle Junior's

German wife Aunt Rita. We knew, however, we made the trip because he had to get to *Boot Hill* Dodge City, Kansas where he said Jesse James and his brother Frank, Cole Younger, Bat Masterson, Pat Garrett, Wyatt Earp and his brothers Morgan and Virgil, and Doc Holliday once rode.

Six of us piled into my father's brown Buick Electra 225 and drove a thousand miles to become a part of Western lore. He took us to Abilene, Kansas to see the Wild West show with the Can-Can Girls with their little skirts flying, and the cowboys in a shoot-out in the streets, and the stage coach coming around the corner with dust flying and guns a-blazin'. The sun was hot, and we were standing there with our eyes buggin' with cowboys falling from the rooftops. My father had arrived. He was living his dream. He was living his television glory.

Any "Western" would satisfy his insatiable desire for what he called a "shoot 'em up." Maybe it was because he was a cowboy at heart and dreamed of one day owning the ranch with the cattle and the horses. Although he was a horseman by profession and was recruited from Warrenton, Virginia because he was the best "hand" this side of the Pecos, he never owned a horse of his own because he was too busy trying to keep shoes on our feet. I was admittedly the worst equestrian in the family; although, my father did teach us all to ride.

He was a cowboy, often wearing his ten gallon hats and slinging his rifles. When my father came through the door, he came home with his guns a blazing and smoke flying. His six shooters were the deadly words that would blast from his mouth. He was our "Marshall," and he was determined he would throw somebody behind bars before the day was over. We followed his law best we could, but more often than not we were the outlaws and would be jailed as a result of our continued lawlessness.

Next to *GunSmoke*, *The Dukes of Hazard* was where my father tuned in. He thought Boss Hog was outrageously funny and Cletus was a sure case of laughs. I was not sure; however, if my dad viewed the show daily because of Bo and Luke Duke or because of the short shorts of Daisy Duke. Whatever the case, my father was the sheriff of our home, and he would make sure we all honored his badge.

When the sheriff, "Marshall Buck," as he might have been more affectionately known, got home with his guns drawn, spurs clanging, and boots stomping, we ran to our safe havens – our rooms, beside our mother, or to one of our baseball, basketball or football practices. He would shoot off one of his words of "Don't you know how to speak when somebody comes in?" or let fire, "Turn that thing off and get up and get these dishes done and that trash out." We would say, "Yes sir," then get out of the way quickly before some harsher words were blasted.

Of course he was right. We should have spoken when he came through the door, but *The Flintstones* overruled our father. We were more interested in Fred and Barney's day at Mr. Slate's rock quarry than in my father's day on "the hill." If it was not the *Flintstones*, it was *Gilligan's Island* that captured our undivided attention. How could he compare to the Skipper and Ginger? He came home from a day of grooming manes, training Open Jumpers, mucking stalls, digging postholes, and cleaning tack and demanded we acknowledge him. When we didn't, he certainly reminded us that we would.

Was he the man of the house because we feared him? Was he the man of the house because he made the most noise? Was he the man of the house because he put a string of profanity together that would make a sailor blush?

Those traits may have been contributing factors in my father's "king of his castle" mentality, but my father was the man of the house because he understood and fulfilled the man's responsibilities. He understood what it was to provide for his family and to "keep" his home.

With five brothers and a sister to grow up with, and as the second oldest in his family, my father learned responsibility early in his life. He left home at sixteen and went West to work on the Santa Anita, Del Mar, and Golden Gate race tracks in California. Then by eighteen he had traveled back East and was in New York working at the Jamaica, Aquaduct, and Saratoga Springs race tracks.

He was a hustler. When he married and had six children to take care of, he would do whatever he had to do to keep food on the table and clothes on their backs. He had neither objections to nor fears of hard work. To him, hard work was a sign of manhood. Hard work was a form of strength. To him, hard work was honorable. And to him, hard work was a truck. A truck represented survival. A truck meant that a person could always haul something, move something, or dump something for cash.

When my father did well with his after hours jobs, we ate well, dressed well, and played well. It is accurately understood that "as the man goes, so goes the home," and as my dad went, so did we. In general, if the man excels, the home excels. If the man elevates, increases, or advances, so does the home. On the other hand, if the man of the house declines, falls, or goes under, so does the home.

God has established the family so that the man is the leader, the "head of the house." Chauvinistic digression is not intended here. I refer to the man as the "head of the house" not as a point of contention with women's liberation or any feminist movement, but as a frame of reference for the godly structure within the home. Call it old fashioned, outdated, or ultra-conservative, but what is certain is that, biblically, the man is the head of the family. God has made men to lead the home. Sure there are times when a woman has to lead her family by design or by dilemma, but the biblical precedent represents man as the leader and head of the house.

> The man of the house is to be the instrument through which God transforms earthly homes into spiritual temples.

Too often men portray an attitude of a domineering, overbearing, forceful, self-centered, authoritarian who is only concerned about one thing – himself. This approach to relationship is not only inappropriate for a healthy marriage and godly family, but it is repulsive and abominable.

The proper biblical lens for viewing a man's role in the family is in Ephesians chapter five. This passage clearly represents the man as the head of the house. That is not to say that the man is the "boss" and everyone must do as he says, or the "dictator" and what he says goes. Neither is the man the "ruler" and everyone under his command. "Head" does not mean boss, dictator, superior, or controller. "Head" is understood in biblical context as the "responsibility carrier." Ephesians 5:23 reminds us "For the husband is the head of the wife, even as Christ is the head of the church: and he is the savior (protector) of the body." Again, "head" means "responsibility carrier."

The husband is the divinely appointed authority of his family and is positioned to be the example of the spiritual life. It is not the aim of the man to collect the treasures of the world. The man of the house is to be the instrument through which God transforms earthly homes into spiritual temples. Likewise, Jesus is the divinely appointed head or authority over His church and demonstrates the nature of God for humanity. Because Jesus is the head of the church, He is responsible for protecting and providing for the welfare of His church. Likewise, the husband is responsible for protecting and providing for the welfare of his family. Moreover, even as Jesus died for the church, the man as the "head" should lay down his life for his family, that is, the husband, as the head, is the "first sacrifice." The man makes the necessary sacrifices for his family's well-being, and gives up whatever is necessary for the promotion of his home.

Anatomically, the head is the signal giver, and what begins in the head is carried out throughout the body. This physiological truth is also represented in any organized structure. Every muscle, limb, appendage, cell, and organ gets its signal from the head. When this physical dynamic is reversed, the body is dysfunctional. The head gives the body its cues, not the body the head, so that what happens with the head happens to the rest of the body. The head gives the signals, the commands, and the instructions to the rest of the body.

What can't be missed are the words of Warren Bennis concerning the leader. He writes, "The leader.....is rarely the brightest person in the group. Rather, they have extraordinary taste, which makes them more curators than creators. They are appreciators of talent and nurturers of talent and they have the ability to recognize valuable ideas." To say the least, most men (husbands) are not the brightest, smartest, or most efficient person in the home, yet, as leader, the man is the curator of talent and the distributor of vision.

The actions in the Garden of Eden are a wonderful example of this role of headship. God set in order the man, Adam, as the head of the home, as the leader of the family. God placed the authority and responsibility of dressing and keeping the Garden not upon Eve, but upon Adam, the man which He had made. God gave Adam the responsibility to "Dress and keep the garden." (Genesis 2:15) Adam was accountable for the garden's upkeep. What cannot be overlooked is that when Adam fell and the Garden

56

became contaminated with sin, God called Adam to give an answer as first position accountability. God did not call Eve in question. God called Adam to the floor and said, "Where art thou Adam?" because Adam was the one held accountable and responsible for all of the activity in the Garden. In short, Adam, who should have been giving the signal as the head to the woman, was instead receiving the signal from the woman. There were not two heads. There was only one person held accountable, called into question – the man, Adam.

Centuries have passed since Adam's irresponsible actions, yet what remains is that the man is still the one that God calls forward and holds first position of responsibility and accountability for what happens in the home. The principle of headship has not changed. That structure has not been modified or altered since the beginning. God is still calling men to the floor and asking them, "Where are you?"

God is asking, "What has happened to the Christian Home?" – and every man is being held accountable. What has happened to the Christian Family where values were taught, and Jesus was mentioned, and prayers were offered, and where folk forgave each other, and worshipped together? What has happened to the home where love was the principle thing, and where nobody was excluded from table? What happened to the home where God was the center of it, and faith was the order of it?" What happened to the family that prayed together, and the family that came to Sunday School together, and the family that went to church together?"

> Men must ascend not to a place of egotism and dominance, but to their spiritual place as the leader in the family.

The indictment upon today's family is simply this: men have not lived up to their responsibilities. Husbands have let down the family. Men must ascend not to a place of egotism and dominance, but to their spiritual place as the leader in the family. Leadership roles in the Christian church and in the family that God desires to be filled by men have been left vacant. Men have aborted their leadership responsibility and have given it to women to fill. When men take their rightful place as leaders in the church and in the home, something profoundly powerful takes place. It is God's design for men to lead, and when men deny their godly design and hand it over to our wives, our sisters, and our mothers we have denied the spiritual truth in which God has made us. We have denied the likeness of God within us to create, to lead, to take dominion, and to direct.

When men take their rightful spiritual places something happens in their homes. When men, as George Whitefield mentions in his book, *The Great Duty of Family Religion*, "act in the three capacities that God has required: as a *prophet*, to instruct; as a *priest*, to pray for and with; and as a *king*, to govern, direct, and provide for them, then our families are the strongest and God most pleased."[1]   As the Apostle Paul declares in ITimothy 5:8, "if any provide not for his own, and specially for those of his own house, he hath denied the faith, and is worse than an infidel." There is no greater degree of apostasy than the man who takes no thought to provide for the spiritual, emotional, mental and physical welfare of his family.

Ignoring the family is never justified. According to I Tim 3:4-5, a man should be "one that ruleth well his own house, having his children in subjection with all gravity. For if a man knows not how to rule his own house, how shall he take care of the church of God?"

I share with you Eight Traits that men should possess to create a better home:

1. Pray – Communicate with God concerning your family. It will be the best time you have ever invested. Prayer is the key to continued strength, vision, and power in the home. If you have children, call out each child's name before the Lord.

2. Protect – Protect your family's reputation. Keep your family name honorable. Protect your family from worldly hazards. Make sure those in your home feel safe and secure physically, mentally, emotionally, and spiritually.

3. Provide – Provide for the needs of your family. Always give to your family the best you can, but know that you will not be able to give them everything. It is not in what you give but why you give it that counts.

4. Practice – Practice what you preach. If you are not willing to do it, don't expect anybody else to do it. Back up your words with action. Your family is depending on you. Or Practice the spiritual disciplines. They will keep you and your family in touch with God. Remember to regularly practice the disciplines of prayer, fasting, worship, meditation, solitude, quiet time, Bible study and Bible reading.

5. Prevent – Prevent negativity in your home. Stop unconstructive behavior at the door. Shut out negativity! Don't let pessimism enter your family.

6. Promote – Promote God in your home. You can't expect anyone else to. Promote your wife and your children, and remember the more you love her, the more your children will respect you. Encourage, encourage, encourage: be the one in the home that others look to for energy, excitement and direction.

7. Promise – Follow through! Make sure you finish what you start, and you do what you say. There is nothing worse than a man that is not true to his word.

8. Prepare – Prepare for the worst but plan for the best. Get ready for the future. Put up pictures of not just your family's past, but put up some pictures of where you want your family to be.

Remember, the man is the head of the house and where the head is going and what the head sees is going to determine the family's future. The man will and can create the home he desires if he follows these traits.

Men are Adam. Husbands are the man of the ground that God wants to fashion with his hands. Men are Adam, and God wants to make something of them. Men are Adam, and God wants to shape them, and form them, and mold them into his image and his likeness. Men are Adam, and are to demonstrate the character of God in the family. Husbands are Adam, and God wants to place dominion in their hands. Husbands, you are Adam, and God wants to put the responsibility of transforming families of men into families of God on your shoulders. Husbands, you are Adam, and God has made you the representation of Christ – you are to "re-present" Christ in the earth. Men, you are Adam, and God has a garden he wants you to dress and keep. Men, you are Adam, and God wants you to stand for him, and carry out the cause of Christ and not fall under pressure.

> God is seeking men who will not compromise the nature of God within them.

The World Needs Men, according to one anonymous writer…
…who cannot be bought

...whose word is there bond
...who put character above wealth
...who possess opinions and a will
...who are larger than their vocations
...who do not hesitate to take chances
...who will not lose their individuality in a crowd
...who will be as honest in small things as in great things
...who will make no compromise with wrong
...whose ambitions are not confined to their own selfish desires
...who will not say they do it "because everybody else does it."
...who are true to their friends through good report and evil report in adversity as well as in prosperity
...who do not believe that shrewdness, cunning, and hard headedness are the best qualities for winning success
...who are not ashamed or afraid to stand for the truth when it is unpopular
...who can say "no" with emphasis, although all the rest of the world says "yes."

According to Psalm 1, men are not to "walk in the counsel of the ungodly, stand in the way of sinners, nor sit in the seat of the scornful, but delight in the law of the Lord." God is seeking men who will not compromise the nature of God within them.

In the book, *For Men Only,* a description of what it takes to be a man is presented by Radio Speaker, David W. Augsburger. He writes:

To be a man
Is to possess the strength to love another,
Not the need to dominate over others.
To be a man
Is to experience the courage to accept another,
Not the compulsion to be an aggressor.
To be a man
Is to keep faith with human values in relationships,
Not to value oneself by position or possessions.
To be a man
Is to be free to give love,
And to be free to accept love in return.[2]

While it is equally true that the description of a man as the "boss," the "dictator," or the "commander" is an inappropriate and improper description of headship, it is also an obscured and faulty view to think that the man as "head of the house" is a "superhero" who is able to "leap tall buildings in a single bound." Men are under a flawed understanding to think that "Head" means, "I've got to make everything work, and I've got to have all the answers."

Men too often live under the misconception that "the man is supposed to keep it all together, and make it all right." But what happens when the bottom drops out? What happens when the man can't control the situations around you? Men make it difficult because men carry the deep burden that we are supposed to be "Mr. Fix-It" and whatever happens the man is the one that is supposed to hold everything together. But what happens when "Mr. Fix-It" needs fixed? Men lean toward an early grave when they think that a man is less than a man if he can't keep the car running, the roof from leaking, the dishwasher working, the grass cut, the money coming in, the tuition paid, the cabinets full, the freezer packed, the closets stuffed, the children happy, and the wife satisfied. Men get bogged down in believing that we are SuperMen. However, that is a task too heavy for any man to carry. Men can't fix it all. Men can't hold it all together. Men don't have all the answers. Men can't, but men are empowered by and serve a God who can, and who is able "to do exceedingly abundantly above, all that we ask or think, according to the power that worketh in us." (Ephesians 3:20)

The husband is the man of the house, but he is not "SuperMan." He is not a comic character with supernatural powers, X-Ray vision, superhuman strength, and supernatural speed, but he is God's man. Too often what women want is a SuperMan – a wonder-working do-everything kind of guy. He is a man that is often times struggling with his place in the world and trying to hold it all together. He is struggling with himself, fighting with his destiny, wrestling with relationships, while hiding from God for the guilt of the past, and waiting and listening for God to speak to him and give him clear direction for his life and for his home.

Adam was hiding from God in the Garden because his world had gotten out of control. He became afraid because he was not able to put it back together. There Adam was hiding behind the bush with his fig leaf on. There Adam was with his world and his woman out of control. There Adam was with his ungrateful, inconsiderate, disobedient self hiding from God. There Adam was hiding thinking that God couldn't see him. There Adam was in total denial of his manhood and in deadly contradiction of his purpose trying to figure out what in the world he was going to do. The fact of the matter is that sometimes men feel just like Adam.

In fact, too often wives approach their husbands like he is supposed to be invincible, indestructible, unstoppable, and unshakeable. However, if men would honestly confess, they would have to admit that to look at them from the outside they appear strong, and built, and buff, on the outside, but inside they are wilted and weak. Men appear invincible, and unstoppable, and indestructible, and unshakeable, while in fact, the most fragile thing in the world is the *male ego*.

Men thrive on performance, and record setting, and speed but have some very sensitive egos. That's why men like to watch baseball, and basketball, and football because men get to watch what most men really want – and that is thousands of people cheering a man on to victory. The male ego needs to be pumped up physically with our muscles bulging, but they also need to be pumped up emotionally. Men want someone to cheer them, somebody to encourage them, somebody to say to them what Gina said to Martin on the television show *Martin*: "You go boy!"

> Every man needs a woman who will be in his corner and not in his face.

Men want someone to cheer them to victory. Every man needs a cheerleader, and guess who that is? – his woman! Every man needs a woman who will be in his corner and not in his face. Every man needs a woman who will be there to support him when he is struggling with failed career, wasted identity, and missed opportunity. Every man needs a woman like Snow White's mirror on the wall who will say, "You are the fairest of them all."

Women have to remember that men are husbands, and fathers, not gods! My personal discovery is that men don't need to be right all the time. Men don't have to be able to do everything. Sometimes women make men think they are superheroes. Men may even act like they have a big red "S" on their chest, but women and men know that's not the case.

Men want to be all powerful and be able to do everything, but unfortunately that's not true. The only reason men want to be able to do everything, and the only reason men even try to do everything is because men are trying to impress the woman. When men don't live up to the challenge, women too often look at him like: "What's wrong with you?" What men need for women to do is remain in his corner regardless of his failures, foibles, or frustrations. Whether men do or do not, the man just needs to hear from the woman say – *not* "Can't you do anything?," – *not* "Will you ever get it together?" – *not* "How long is it going to take this time?" – but "I'm in your corner, and I've got your back!"

What is profound is when Adam was at his lowest, most miserable moment, and kicked out of paradise Eve was right there with him. Eve stuck with her man in spite of the adversity he faced. What men need to know is that when we fail, when we "lose paradise," that our woman is still there with us. William Lyon Phelps said it well, "Every man who is happy at home is a successful man, even if he has failed in everything else." Men don't need or want the nagging, the complaining, the "neck rolls" with glazed attitude, and the finger pointing from their spouse. What the husband needs to know is that his wife is still the "rib by his side" and not a "thorn in his flesh."

Too often a woman will be with the man as long as he is in paradise, but the moment he hits bottom, or the moment he loses his income and goes from riches to rags, she can't deal with him. The woman often equates his manhood with the size of his paycheck. Manhood is not determined by the size of the man's salary, the year and make of his car, the fabric in his suit, or on which floor is his office. Manhood is determined by the willingness to fulfill God's will and the courage to be you.

The poem, *If,* by Rudyard Kipling, offers a driving example of what it takes to be a man.

If you can keep your head when all about you
Are losing theirs and blaming it on you;
If you can trust yourself when all men doubt you,
But make allowance for their doubting too;
If you can wait and not be tired by waiting,
Or, being lied about, don't deal in lies,
Or, being hated, don't give way to hating,
And yet don't look too good, nor talk too wise;

If you can dream - and not make dreams your master;
If you can think - and not make thoughts your aim;
If you can meet with triumph and disaster
And treat those two imposters just the same;
If you can bear to hear the truth you've spoken
Twisted by knaves to make a trap for fools,

Or watch the things you gave your life to broken,
And stoop and build 'em up with wornout tools;

If you can talk with crowds and keep your virtue,
Or walk with kings - nor lose the common touch;
If neither foes nor loving friends can hurt you;
If all men count with you, but none too much;
If you can fill the unforgiving minute
With sixty seconds' worth of distance run -
Yours is the Earth and everything that's in it,
And - which is more - you'll be a Man my son!

In a marital relationship, what impacts one spouse impacts the other. When God made man and woman to be husband and wife, he patterned them to be "one" physically, emotionally and spiritually. Genesis 1:27 declares, "God created man in his own image, in the image of God created he him; male and female created he them. And God blessed them." "Blessed" in this passage of scripture not only means "to bestow a gift," but "blessed" also means "to assign a function. Then in Genesis 2:24 it says, "Therefore shall a man leave his father and his mother, and shall cleave unto his wife: and they shall be one flesh." God said the two become one, which suggests that Man and Woman, husband and wife are not Singles but EQUALS. They are Equal in Respect, Equal in Dignity, Equal in Importance, Equal in Spirituality, Equal in God, Equal in Intelligence, Equal in Character. Yet, notice that when the scripture speaks of "them" it speaks of "them" as distinct, as male and female, which suggests that they may be EQUAL, but they are not IDENTICAL.

The man and the woman are not identical physically, emotionally, or functionally. Men and women run off of different fuels. Men are Diesel powered; women are Gasoline powered. Neither are Men and Women identical in their roles. Men and women were designed of God to carry out different functions, and as a result men and women see things in different ways.

64

Here is an interesting table to review the differences between men and women.

MEN	WOMEN
Husbands are Exothermic	Wives are Endothermic
Men Heat up from outside in	Women heat up from inside out
Men are heady	Women are hearty
Men think it	Women feel it
Men tend to look for success	Women tend to look for security
Men tend to be Providers	Women tend to be Nurturers.
Men are hunters	Women are healers.

Loving the Lord is essential to any healthy marriage. Everything else is secondary – cars, cash and clothes don't make a marriage go or grow. When two people come together and love each other as God loves them, the marriage is fit for strength, soundness and success. The marriage, with God's presence, becomes a blessed union and not a continual brawl.

Marriage is a COMPLIMENTARY relationship not a COMPETITIVE relationship. We are to be the *compliment of* each other, not to the *competition between* each other. That's why the Bible says in Genesis 1:18, "It is not good for the man to be alone; I will make a help MEET for him." The word "Meet" is *suitable* for him, or better yet, *complimentary* to him. Everybody wants to know who rules, who runs the house, and who is in control. When the relationship is a competitive one, then "power struggles" are the order of the day. It is not a matter of which person is most important or which one is the greatest. That is the wrong

understanding within the relationship. It's not about a
husband being over his wife in some dictatorial fashion but the
complimentary relationship between husband and wife is about
being able to view the function of the home from two different
perspectives to create one awesome vision and revelation of God.

The relationship of husband and wife is not about "who wears
the pants in the family," but is to be understood more as a lock and
key, or a bow and arrow. It is useless to ask which is more
important or which is the greater, the lock or the key, the bow or the
arrow because one is ineffective without the other. Both need the
other to fulfill their greatest function.

Men would do well to duplicate the manner of President
Obama as he spoke on his role as husband/father with marked
clarity: "My wife has been my closest friend, my closest advisor.
And...she's not somebody who looks to the limelight, or even is
wild about me being in politics. And that's a good reality check on
me. When I go home, she wants me to be a good father and a good
husband. And everything else is secondary to that." Men would be
wise to take President Obama's lead, and let everything become
secondary to being a good husband and a good father. If we men
get that right, we will have gained not only our families, but also
every good thing in the world.

Chapter VI

Wonder Woman

"A hundred men may make an encampment, but it takes a woman to make a home."

– Chinese Proverb

"Who can find a virtuous woman, for her price is far above rubies?"

– Proverbs 31:10

The days of "Big Momma" are gone. The typically overweight grandmother that cooked up the pot of turnip greens, made the southern fried chicken, shared the wisdom for life's turbulence, and became the buffer between parents and children has become a thing of the past. She has become a relic forever immortalized in the archives of Black culture. By the end of my generation, "Big Mommas" had been placed on the endangered species list and were rapidly being replaced with "Little Mommas"– the young single parent mother who was inexperienced in life and unaware of responsibility.

While "Big Momma" nurtured her children and cheered them to success, "Little Momma" struggled to be a momma and find her place in the world. While "Big Momma" caressed everyone that came around her and smothered them in her bosom, "Little Momma" crossed her eyes, rolled her neck and was likely to expose her bosom.[1] While "Big Momma" was keeping the family grounded in godly wisdom, "Little Momma" seemed to have an edge about her as if she had been mistreated or misguided and didn't know how to redirect her life for positive progress. While

68

"Big Momma" embraced all children as her own, "Little Momma" had two or three children and each child had a different daddy.

Big Momma was gone and Little Momma surfaced; however, in either case Momma became the cornerstone of the home. She was the piece of the family that God positioned to sustain the home. Left to men, the home would be little more than a sports center or cigar bar, but mothers had the godly intuition and know how to turn a house into a home.

Although the Holy Scriptures don't speak of "Big" or "Little" momma, there is posted in the Bible for every family the description of what mothers should be. The glory of the virtuous woman is distinctively identified in Genesis chapter 2 and Proverbs chapter 31. In Genesis chapter 2 the woman has been designed of God as the queen of God's creation. She is described as being elegant in her frame, sculptured in her figure, and unique in her femininity. In Proverbs chapter 31 God has endowed her with the tenderness of humanity, and has presented the virtuous woman as a warm, loving, and industrious soul who takes care of her home, loves her children and honors her husband.

Proverbs chapter 31 demonstrates what the virtuous woman does, while Genesis chapter 2 defines who the virtuous woman is. She is Eve, and she is defined as the "mother of all living." She is the last of God's creation and the carrier of life. She is the one that would carry redemption in her womb and deliver salvation to the world.

This mark of distinction has not changed. Every woman, along with so many other identifiers, is still a carrier of redemption and a giver of life. No wonder a mother is the last to give up on her children no matter how disruptive, disoriented, or discouraged her children may be. Through the woman the restoration of the world would come. The Bible literally speaks of Eve in Genesis 3:15 as carrying the seed that will bruise the head of Satan, that is, that will ultimately defeat the Devil.

In addition to the mother of all living, Eve is also the first wife in creation. She was designed to be the "help meet" to her husband. As recorded in Genesis 2:18, "the Lord God said, it is not good that the man should be alone; I will make him an help meet for him." "Help meet" is the supportive role of defender, helper, and number one advisor to the husband. The word "help" literally

comes from the Hebrew word *ezer* (ay-zer) which means
to "help," to "surround," to "protect," to "aid."
    As God said to Adam, so God said to my father, "I will make
him a help meet for him." My mother was the "help meet" for my
father. As mentioned in the Nelson Study Bible, the word *meet*
"conveys the idea of aiding someone in need....'Meet' comes from
the Hebrew word meaning 'opposite.' Literally it is 'according to
the opposite of him,' meaning that she will complement and
correspond to him."[2]
    In order for the man to fulfill his function, he would need
help, and the woman became the aid suitable for the man to fulfill
his function. Eve was intended for Adam to be the person he could
lean on, talk to, walk with, and work for.
    Woman was truly made of God in the style and words of
Maya Angelou's poetic feminine description:

Pretty women wonder where my secret lies.
I'm not cute or built to suit a fashion model's size
    But when I start to tell them,
    They think I'm telling lies.
    I say,
    It's in the reach of my arms
        The span of my hips,
        The stride of my step,
        The curl of my lips.
    I'm a woman
        Phenomenally.
        Phenomenal woman.
        That's me.

    My mother was a phenomenal woman, and she was also my
father's help-meet. She was made for him. She was extremely
talented, and I thought she could do anything, that is, anything to
get on my father's nerves when he was trying to finish one of his
million and one projects. Her specialty, it seemed, was telling my
dad not what to do but how to do it. There never was a project that
my dad tackled – from fixing the sink, snaking out the sewer drain,
planting a garden, to loading a truck full of furniture, hauling
discarded aluminum siding, trimming the neighbor's hedges, or
digging post holes for a fence – that my mother wasn't looking over
his shoulder instructing him on the right way to get the job done.
    The point of my mother's unrelenting advice became the point
at which my father had taken all he could and would begin to add

some expletives to his language that was not fit for young boys or old men. When my father's frustrations had reached their limit, he would begin to cuss like a sailor. In fact, if sailors could cuss, my father was the whole Navy. He could launch some four letter words in between what he was trying to say that would be a mile long. Sometimes his profanity would be like explosive missiles and at other times he would use them like rapid fire artillery. Nonetheless, he became known for his illustrative language and didn't care who heard.

My mother didn't pay much attention to his blasphemously colorful language and gave him her advice anyway. The unusual part was that more often than not her advice was right. He always rejected her advice for the alternative – doing it his way. It might have taken him an extra hour or two according to his methods, but he was determined to show her that there was more than one person in the family that could do the job.

Yet, in all of the disagreements and disputes, my mother and father were the Adam and Eve, the match that God had made for each other. She became the completion of my father, finishing his sentences, clearing his plates, and finalizing his projects. They were the "Fred and Wilma Flintstones," the "Edith and Archie Bunkers," the "George and Weezie Jeffersons" of our home.

My father was not complete without my mother, just as Adam was not complete without Eve. God could have made Eve from the dust of the ground as He did Adam, but instead God made the woman from the rib of the man to symbolize their oneness in love and life.

Amazingly, inasmuch as Adam, the man, was the glory of God's creation, Eve, the woman, was the glory of man, as she was taken out of him. Eve's life was literally taken out of Adam, which suggests that the life of the husband and wife is one. While the man and the woman are two separate individuals, uniquely, the husband and wife are one complimentary union. In Genesis 2:23-24, Adam goes so far as to describe this remarkable union with Eve as literally being, "bone of my bones, and flesh of my flesh...therefore shall a man leave his father and mother, and shall cleave unto his wife: and *they shall be one flesh.*"

Before moving on, what must not be overlooked is that Eve, the woman, represents the church of Jesus Christ. As Adam represents Jesus Christ – the head of the church, so Eve represents the Church – the bride of Christ. The wife is the means through which new life is birthed into the world, and the church is the avenue through which new life is birthed into the kingdom of God.

As mentioned in the last chapter, the man and the woman are one, yet men and women are *equal* but not *identical*. This is as obvious as viewing the physical and physiological makeup of the man and the woman. It is apparent that men and women are not identical.

The role of the husband and wife within the family is not to be approached in terms of a *competitive* relationship but as a *complimentary* union. It is absurd to talk about the man and woman as one being superior and the other inferior, or as a tiered household of greater and lesser, superior and subordinate. Just as men and women are the perfect fit physically, they are also the perfect fit emotionally. The compliment in personality is extraordinary. In contemporary terms men have been described as being from Mars and women as coming from Venus,[3] suggesting that there are fundamental physical, psychological, and emotional differences between men and women.

As I mentioned in the last chapter husbands heat up from the outside in – from visual/external stimuli, and women heat up from the inside out, from emotional/internal stimuli. Men and women even approach the engagement of relationship differently. For example, a man typically gives love/romance to get sex, and a woman typically gives sex to get love/romance. They are two complimentary souls after the same end, but they approach that end from two different perspectives.

My point is this: the husband and wife are not two separate and independent persons functioning in isolation from each other; they are one complimentary body in mission and in motion. The moment a man and a woman say, "I Do," *individuality* merges into *solidarity*. They become one. There is a personal merger of goals, objectives, values, time, planning, finances, and bodies. Above all there is a merger of mission, which will be examined later in this chapter.

The husband and wife are one, and they are a team working together to form family. Yet, a woman's role within the family is distinct. She functions within the family unlike the man. She operates with a style and sensitivity that is unmatched by her husband. She performs with a grace and a flare that is uncompromised. She lives with a softness and a tenderness that is unequaled. She walks with a confidence and a concern that is unquestionable.

In fact, wives have historically performed in ways to sustain the family that have baffled any man. Through world wars and economic depressions, natural disasters and political overthrows, slavery and civil rights movements, riots and underground missions, layoffs and corporate downsizings, the woman has kept the family together.

I call wives "Wonder Women" because in this twenty-first century, during economic recession, housing foreclosures, and Banking Bail-Outs, women have succeeded in raising their children, supporting their man, and standing up for their rights. Even when men are locked behind bars having become dead beat dads, the secure woman of the home is still holding the family together. If the man is the "Head" of the house, then a declaration is made that the woman is the "Backbone" of the home.

When bills needed paid, the family needed fed, the money needed to be stretched, the babies needed nursed, the woman has acted like Wonder Woman. The woman of the house would take a piece of material, a needle, and some thread, and what looked like rags to some, would end up being a quilt, some curtains, or dress for school. She would take in children that weren't hers and raise them as her own and the children never knew the difference. She would iron clothes, wash dishes, sweep floors, scrub toilets, so that she could have a few extra pennies to save so that her babies one day could go to college. She was the personification of the late seventies Enjoli perfume commercial:

I can put the wash on the line,
 Feed the kids, get dressed,
Pass out the kisses
 And get to work by five to nine.
I can bring home the bacon
 Fry it up in the pan
And never, never, never let you forget you're a man...
 Cause I'm a woman!

Unfortunately, instead of embracing the woman's talents, men too often have become intimidated by their skills. A woman's abilities often make a man uncomfortable. Men have become intimidated by a woman's successes, frustrated by her accomplishments, embittered by her achievements, distraught by her skills, overwhelmed by her expertise, aggravated by her talents, annoyed by her competence, bothered by her creativity, and disturbed by her ingenuity. Men let the woman's ambition to "be somebody" stifle their appreciation of her. She gets a job, and the man gets upset. She gets a degree, and the man doesn't know how to deal with her. She gets a promotion, and the man is stymied.

For many men the empowered woman has become their fiercest nightmare. Too many men lose confidence, become inhibited, run away and hide their masculinity as a result of the empowered woman. Isn't that what Adam did when Eve became selfishly empowered? Adam hid from God but ran from the woman. The career woman can be overwhelming. The man doesn't know how to love her because while she has determined to make something of her life, he has largely decided to do nothing with his.

The bottom line is Super Man and Wonder Woman must work together to make the best and most powerful marital relationship. As the lock is useless without the key and the bow is unproductive without the arrow, so the man is ineffective without the woman. Neither can create the strength needed to keep a marriage together on their own.

The man and the woman have to work equally as hard to make the marriage as strong as it can be remembering that love is never a fifty-fifty proposition. The formula for right relationship is not each giving a half to make a whole relationship. But more accurately, the husband and wife must give one hundred percent of themselves to make one healthy marital relationship. Any part held back and the relationship never reaches its full potential. Love has to be two people giving one hundred percent.

Here is my **Recipe for a Happy Marriage:**

Ingredients
   1 Strong man
   1 Secure woman
   2 loving hearts

3 pounds of forgiveness
A gallon of Prayer (added daily)
Equal parts Giving and Sacrifice
A heap of patience
A cup of humility
¾ cup of Understanding
A Sense of humor (to taste)
A splash of "want-to"
A cup of "for-your-eyes-only"
½ tablespoon of perseverance
1 teaspoon of "whatever-it-takes"
1 common desire
Time (as much as you've got)
1 Loving Savior

Preparation:
Take one strong man and one secure woman, extract their two loving hearts and mix them thoroughly over time. Let marinate in prayer. Add love, forgiveness, patience, and some sense of humor (to taste). Mix in slowly common desire, then fold in humility with equal parts of giving and sacrifice. Beat in understanding. Add a splash of "want-to" and a cup of "for-your-eyes-only." Heat to boiling with perseverance; add "whatever-it-takes." Cover with one Savior. Never serve with bad attitude.

Serves: a lifetime.

Happy marriages are not automatic. They come by hard work and constant care. Marriage takes an equally and permanently committed man and woman to make it work. While the woman is recognizing the man as the head and being submissive to him, men are to be cherishing, loving, and honoring her. Space will not allow me to explore the scriptures in I Peter 3:7, Genesis chapter 2, The Song of Solomon, and Proverbs 31 that speak of honoring the woman. What bears repeating, however, is that as the man is the glory of God, the woman is the glory of man. Men are never to treat the woman less than she was intended to be thought of because in so doing the man diminishes his own glory. For a man to call a woman out of her name or to mistreat her is to speak derogatorily and negatively toward himself.

The man would have been incomplete without the woman. As God made man, He made Adam perfect in his humanity. Unfortunately, Adam was incomplete in his identity. For Adam to fully understand who he was as a person and as a man, he needed another person of his human kind. It was not good for Adam to be alone because he would not have fully understood his function as a man, so God created a woman, the perfect compliment to Adam's masculinity. Without Eve, Adam's identity would have been incomplete. Through the woman, the man gained greater understanding of himself.

One of the best descriptions of this reciprocal relationship is in I Peter 3:5-7, which says:

> For this is the way the holy women of the past
> who put their hope in God used to make them-
> selves beautiful. They were submissive to
> their own husbands, like Sarah, who obeyed
> Abraham and called him her master. You are
> her daughters if you do what is right and do not
> give way to fear. Husbands, in the same way
> be considerate as you live with your wives, and
> treat them with respect as the weaker partner
> and as heirs with you of the gracious gift of life,
> so that nothing will hinder your prayers.[4]

Peter does not imply by calling the woman the weaker vessel any moral or intellectual inferiority. What Peter suggests by calling the woman the "weaker" vessel is not suggesting moral or intellectual inferiority, but he is recognizing the woman's physical limitations. The word "weaker" comes from the Greek word *asthenes* (as-then-ace), which means "strengthless, more feeble, weak." The *Life Application Bible* explains the treatment of a man toward a woman this way: "A man who honors his wife as a member of the weaker sex will protect, respect, help, and stay with her. He will not expect her to work full-time outside and full-time at home; he will lighten her load wherever he can. He will be sensitive to her needs, and he will relate to her with courtesy, consideration, insight, and tact."[5]

This adoration of women is strongly emphasized in Ephesians 5:22, 25, 28, 29. It is written:

> Wives, be subject to your own husbands, as to the
> Lord. …Husbands love your wives, just as Christ
> loved the church and gave Himself for her…So
> husbands ought also to love their wives as their own

bodies. He who loves his own wife loves himself;
For no one ever hated his own flesh; but nourishes
and cherishes it, just as the Christ does the church.[6]

Women are spoken of here as being adored and cherished by the husband. The focal point is on the word "submit." After the husband and wife submit to God, the woman submits to her husband while the husband loves, honors, and adores her. The word submission is a dirty word in many marriages and for many wives. It's the word that many women don't want to hear and many men want to emphasize that has damaged too many marriages. But the word submission is not as intimidating as it may appear. The word submission, however, is a wonderful representation of what a marriage is intended to be.

Etymologically, the word "submission" is made up of the word *mission* and the prefix *sub*. The prefix "Sub" means "under," and attached to the word mission simply means "coming under one mission." What cannot be overlooked in the Ephesian 5 text is that healthy, godly marital relationship begins with the husband and the wife submitting to each other in the fear of God (verse 17). That mutual submission to each other and the resounding reverence toward God determines the one mission which is God's mission for the relationship.

The hazard in many relationships is that the husband and wife are on two or more different missions, but a healthy marriage consists of one mission and both the man and the woman falling under that assignment. Every marriage needs to have a Mission Statement answering the questions:
(1) What is it that God has given us to do?
(2) For what purpose did God create this holy union?
(3) What is our major assignment from God?
(4) What is it that we will look back on after our lives have ended and say we have completed together?

Remember, it is possible for the husband and wife to have individual secondary missions, but there will be one primary mission that the couple has to unite together to complete. (Hint: You will know what your marital mission is when you realize it could not and it cannot be completed without your spouse. If you can complete it on your own, it is not your marital mission.)

Here are seven tips for women on interacting with their husbands.

1. **Help** – Help him; don't humor him. He wants a woman that will cheer him to victory not challenge him in pursuit. He can do it himself; he just needs you to support him.
2. **Hold** – Hold him; he needs to know that you are there for him, not a threat to him.
3. **Handle** – Handle him with care. His ego is more fragile than you think.
4. **Hear** – Hear him; hear what he has to say without response. Perfect the art of hearing what he doesn't say – it is usually what he doesn't say that counts.
5. **Highlight** – Highlight your feminine qualities. He wants a woman that maintains her feminine appeal from the inside out. He will appreciate that more than anything else.
6. **Huddle** – Know that he likes calling the play, although, you may still have to score the points. You do it, but make him think he did.
7. **Honor** – Honor his work, his ability, his presence. After all, he is driven by respect.

In a book titled, *Preparing for Your Marriage*, by William J. McRae, the use of the word Submission in the marital relationship is explained this way: "Submission does not justify suppression by your husband but does imply obedience to and respect for your husband."[7] No biblical text implies or suggests that a woman is to be dominated. I must repeat that no where in the Holy Scriptures does God's word imply or suggest that a woman is to be viewed or treated as less than the glory she is. The wife is not a doormat to be walked on. Submission is not meant to dampen the qualities and contributions of the wife but to highlight them in the glory of a mutual love between the man and the woman.

McRae continues, "Submission does not stifle your leadership, creativity, and initiative as a wife."[8] The woman has just as much to offer the relationship as the man. The issue is that she should always offer it as a response to the love she has been given. In that way the wife will make decisions with, make arguments for, and participates in discussions about the family as the helper that God intended. I agree wholeheartedly with McRae that "It is not only the wife's right but also her responsibility to function as a partner in this partnership. Every Christian husband should consult his wife as his closest advisor and make decisions with her interests in view."[9]

Marriage is a "Team" effort, and every husband should approach his wife as the continuation and extension of himself. **T.E.A.M.** is **Treating Each As Meaningful**. Neither person is shunned or despised for their particular skills, talents or abilities, but there is a mutual appreciation of the other's contribution.

A woman wants to know that her total person is appreciated and respected, even the deepest parts of her being (her mind, her soul, her spirit). If the man wants the woman to *submit* to him, to have a voluntary inner attitude of respect and trust toward him, love must be the endearing and enduring quality in the relationship. Without love, submission quickly becomes dominance and manipulation. She becomes an "object" for him to enjoy, no more than a toy for him to find his own delight, and God never intended for the man to dominate his woman but to elevate her. She wants to know that all of who she is is enjoyed and treated with tenderness and respect not because of a "manipulative desire that hopes to get from her what will bring pleasure to him."[10]

A woman wants a man to be "*into her*" not just "into her." She needs him to see her not as an object to be used but as a person to be loved and treated with affection and gentleness. Once she knows he wants her for more than her body and her beauty, for something more than a trophy bride and a piece of eye candy, she will give him her all and do anything for him.

Too many men are still playing "the game." All they want, even in the marital relationship, is to look at her as an object for his consumption and as an article for his use, so he wines her, and dines her, and then takes her home and expects for her to "put out" for what he has invested in. Women, you are not a blue chip stock to be brokered. Every man has to understand that a woman today can do for herself. There is a level of independence about her that is unprecedented. Today's woman can do well by herself. She doesn't need a man to give her anything but mutual respect and admiration.

As a result of this male endearing dominance, women have come to doubt the authenticity of a man's love. She has learned from a young age that men will use her and think nothing of her, so in self defense she guards her heart, as well as, her body from her advancing predator. Once again Crabb reminds us:

> In a fallen world, she learns that offering all
> that she is to another runs the terrible risk
> of rejection and abuse. And because she too
> is fallen and therefore committed to her own
> well-being with no thought of dependence on
> God, she figures out how to minimize the risks
> by hiding the tenderest parts of her soul and
> avoiding an honest look at her ugly parts.[11]

What do you think the fig leaf was about? And men wonder why she can be so rough, and sometimes as hard as nails, and why a woman frequently has an edge about her because "In order to survive in a world where people carelessly hurt her and use her for their own purposes, she learns to cover her delicate nature with a hard crust, a toughness always on the alert for dangers."[12] She says like Sophia in the movie *The Color Purple*, "All my life I had to fight. I had to fight my uncles, had to fight my daddy. And God knows before I let Harpo beat me...I'd kill him dead." When she is by her self long enough to reflect on what she really wants, she becomes at least vaguely aware (sometimes acutely to the point of despair) of how nice it would be if someone were tough for her."[13]

A woman does not want a mouse but a man for a husband. She wants a man who will commit to her and who is not afraid to become deeply involved with her mentally, emotionally, spiritually, and physically, and who is not intimidated by her mind and abilities, and who offers direction in relationship, and will protect and defend her honor. The woman is looking for someone who will support her, be her advocate. She is not looking for somebody to control her; she is looking for somebody who will free her to be all of what God has gifted her to be.

> Deep within her being, she longs for an advocate,
> not a tyrant who would control her life with his
> strength. She is looking for an advocate whose
> strength on her behalf would free her to go "off
> duty" and to express more of who she really is.[14]

The husband doesn't tell his wife enough how much she means to him. Men usually wait till after the relationship is damaged or divorced before they try to articulate what is really in his heart. Men would do well to heed the words of the poet:

> *Tell Her So:*
> *Amid the cares of married life,*
> *In spite of toil and business strife,*
> *If you value your sweet wife,*
> *Tell her so!*
>
> *There was a time you thought it bliss*
> *To get the favor of a kiss;*
> *A dozen now won't come amiss –*
> *Tell her so!*
>
> *Don't act as if she's passed her prime,*
> *As though to please her were a crime –*
> *If e'er you loved her, now's the time;*
> *Tell her so!*
>
> *You are hers and hers alone;*
> *Well you know she's all your own;*
> *Don't wait to carve it on the stone –*
> *Tell her so!*
>
> *Never let her heart grow cold;*
> *Richer beauties will unfold.*
> *She is worth her weight in gold;*
> *Tell her so!*
> -- Author Unknown

All a woman wants is for a man to "Tell Her So." Yet, the man, whether stubborn or stupid, ceases to provide the affirmations necessary to offer his wife the dignity she deserves. She is a woman, and a **W.O.M.A.N.** is **W**hat **O**ther **M**en **A**lways **N**otice.

The problem is that too often the husband doesn't notice his wife, but other men do. She changes her hairstyle, and he doesn't realize it. She buys a new dress, and he pays no attention. She loses twenty pounds, and he gives it no regard. She prepares a great meal, and he fails to recognize. Husbands don't give wives the attention they need and deserve. It is interesting that men will notice every woman except for their own.

What do men do when they begin to see beyond the outer layer of a woman's inviting exterior and the phenomenal woman surfaces? How does he respond to a woman that amazes him with all the deeper intricacies of her life? What does he do when commitment is on the line, and she needs to know that he is there for her and not her body? What does he do when she begins to invite him into a meaningful relationship with the confidence that there really was something special about her? What do we do when she says, "I love you." The man says, "Now, now, Hold on...Hold on...I ain't said all that. We need to take our time here." Because he is scared of what commitment will bring and what saying "yes" will do, he backs off and refuses to commit. He is unaware that giving his "all" to her will expose him to a level of his manhood that would have been forever buried under mounds of fear and disappointment. Adam was perfect in his humanity but incomplete in his identity until Eve came on the scene. Only then, did Adam know who he really was, and what lay deeper inside of him. The woman brought the best out of him.

Men say women are too emotional, too smothering, too moody – "I can't get too involved." Women are not moody; they just need to be understood because while men see love represented in respect, women see love represented in security. A woman, for example, can get mad one minute and thirty minutes later and be as pleasant as peach pie and act like nothing is wrong? A man, on the other hand, will get angry and stay that way for two or three days. It is because men have what is called *Sustained Aggression.* It is part of our primitive nature as hunters. When men went out for the kill, men had to be able to sustain their aggression over three, four or five days until they made a kill on the hunt. Men had to sustain their aggression. On the other hand, women had to learn that when they got angry or upset, they had to come down quickly for the health of their babies because sustained aggression with the female caused a decrease in their milk production with the lactate glands and would cause a less nourished baby when they nursed from their mothers. As a result of this physiological phenomenon, mothers had to learn to get upset then regroup quickly for the health of her babies.

In general, women come down and gather themselves quickly to help keep us, children and their men, settled and focused. They help maintain balance in our lives. When the man can't hold it together and make it work, the woman is able to bring calmness to the table that raises perspective, introduces hope, and makes everything all right. There is a transformative quality that women bring to the table. It is the impact of a woman's touch. Her touch is transformative. Her presence is healing. Her words are calming. Her look is motivating. And her smile is illuminating.

82

What wives do for men is redistribute the bad and make a bad situation better. Women are able to reel men back in when men have gone too far off track. Women bring the "woman's touch."

Don't let the great lyrics of James Brown fool you. He sang, "This is a Man's World," and that may or may not be true, but a woman's presence makes even the roughest of times sweeter. Men ought to appreciate her and say, "That's my girl!" She makes even the saddest of moments bright. That's my girl! She makes even the dullest of times exciting. That's my girl! She offers hope in despair. That's my girl! *The Temptations* sang of the importance of a woman and their significance in making any dull situation exciting and refreshing when they harmonized the tune:

> I've got sunshine
> On a cloudy day
> When it's cold outside
> I've got the month of May.
> Well, I guess you'll say
> What can make me feel this way?
> My girl, (My Girl, my girl)
> Talkin' 'bout my girl. (My girl)

Chapter VII

No Ring Master

"Be who you are and say what you feel because those who mind don't matter and those who matter don't mind."
— Dr. Seuss

"And Adam knew Eve his wife: and she conceived, and bare Cain, and said, I have gotten a man from the Lord."
— Genesis 4:1

"Remember now thy creator in the days of thy youth."
— Ecclesiastes 12:1

Chaos was welcomed in our home. In fact, it often seemed like the more people running through the house, the more chicken being fried, the more noise being made, the more people looking for a seat, the better. We were often called "the fun house," the place of perpetual excitement.

With six children filling the house and each child having their host of friends scavenging through the cupboard looking for a peanut butter or a tuna fish sandwich, there was never a dull moment in our home. No matter who it was that stopped by, our idea of hospitality was to feed them whether they wanted it or not. To our friends, our home was their home. Whatever we had they had, and whatever we ate they ate. It didn't matter what time of the day or night; we were always raising the roof or raiding the refrigerator.

A circus we were not; we had no ring master – we were a zoo. The only difference between us and the gorillas and tigers at the zoo

84

was that we were not, could not, and would not be caged. We roamed freely in our individual mischief and with every child, my mother would say, came greater joy. My mother would agree with the words of Sidonie Gruenberg: "Home is the place where boys and girls first learn how to limit their wishes, abide by rules, and consider the rights and needs of others."

One of the great joys of family is being able to bring children into the world. I asked my mother why she stopped at bearing six children, and she said, "I would have had more, but my body wouldn't let me." I could only imagine growing up with a younger brother or sister to push around and offer the finer details of life.

God's instruction to Adam and Eve was to populate the earth with others of their kind. According to their Genesis 1:27 responsibility, Adam and Eve were given the glorious instruction "to be fruitful and multiply." By the joining of their bodies as a picture of the joining of their love for each other in physical intercourse, they would produce another living, breathing, thinking, speaking human being. By their union, another person would be born in their image and in their likeness.

God gave the world's first parents the unusual ability to become like Him and be procreators in the world. As Adam was made in the image of God, so the next generation of human beings would be made in their image: God the Creator, Adam and Eve the procreators. They received the generative power to reproduce after their kind. Like every other living thing that had the seed of the next generation within it, so Adam would carry the seed of man's next generation within him. The seed of that which is to come is within that which already is.

Genesis 4:1 says, "And Adam knew his wife Eve and she conceived, and bare Cain" – the first child, the next generation of human beings upon the earth. She bare Cain – the first promise of God fulfilled. She bare Cain – Eve's baby boy. She bare Cain – the embodied expression of love between Adam and Eve. Cain was Adam's seed – the future prospect to carry the promise of God and the baby boy that was to turn their fallen situation around and return them to paradise. Cain was God's gift to Adam and Eve. He was Adam and Eve's greatest earthly responsibility – Eve's first child.

Every child is an original masterpiece.

The words Eve speaks when her baby was born are striking. As Cain is delivered, Eve says in Genesis 4:1, "I have gotten a man from the Lord." Like any mother and father what joy must have filled their home when she gave birth to a baby boy. How proud they must have been to know that God had found favor with them to birth a son. How pleased she must have been to have delivered a healthy baby boy with ten toes, and ten fingers, and beautiful eyes.

Eve said, "I have gotten a man from the Lord." Don't miss the words "*from the Lord.*" The phrase suggests this child is God's gift, as God "gave." In fact, every life that comes into this world is a gift from God. Every newborn is God's investment in humanity. Every time a child is born the child reminds us that God hasn't given up on us. God is still giving life. "Eve sees her generative power," as one commentator mentions, "as part of the sharing of divine power: she says, 'Yahweh formed man: I have formed the second man'."[1]

Every child is a gift from God with dignity and value, with possibility and worth. Every child is given from God with life and expression, and personality, and distinction, and uniqueness regardless of their social status, physical condition, racial description, or genetic makeup. Every child is an original masterpiece.

No child is illegitimate. Every child is legitimate before God. The child didn't perform any criminal act and was not an accomplice in any unlawful event in their arrival. It's not the child's fault that sometimes they are birthed out of and into irresponsible relationships. The relationship in which they were produced may not be justifiable, but the child is acceptable and authenticated in the sight of God. The child has just as much right and reason to be here as anyone else that has been given the breath of life. Every child, regardless of how they arrived, deserves to love and be loved.

Eve gave birth again and bare Abel. This was Cain's brother to love and embrace. Yet, when each son brought an offering to God, God received the offering of Abel and not of Cain. As a result of God's refusal of Cain's offering, Cain's anger turned to rage, and Cain murdered Abel.

This first murder scene disturbs all of humanity. Brother killing brother! They were out in the field preparing an offering before God when one became at odds with the other. Hate filled the heart of Cain and momma and daddy were sitting back unaware of what's going on. The world's first family is in total chaos. The world's first family is killing each other and has become a bloody dysfunctional family.

The question to be raised is: If every child is from God, then why do they do such crazy things? If every child is from God, why do they hate? Why do they fight with their brother? Why do they kill each other? Why is their rivalry between them? The answer lies within their parental descriptions.

The problem with Cain killing Abel is the same problem that every child has, and that is, as parents, there is some of us in them. The problem is not that they have challenges to meet, and difficulties to face, and issues to deal with. The problem is that they have their parents' DNA. They have their parents' genes. Cain slew Abel, and that behavior was imbedded in him from his mother and father: to be rebellious, relentless, disobedient, jealous, envious, and unappreciative.

Parents shouldn't be too upset with their children when their children act out because they are only acting upon what their parents have put in them. Parents shouldn't be too disappointed with their children when they cuss the teacher out because their children are only imitating what they've seen their parents do. Parents shouldn't scold them too harshly when they are fighting in school because they are only copying the behavior they see in their parents. So much of a child's behavior is a behavior they learned from their parents. It's not them – it's us.

Children follow their parents' example. Children do what they see their parents do. If parents aren't going to live according to proper values, make right decisions, follow God's commandments, and surrender to God's will, then how can children be expected to? "To do as I say not as I do" does not work. In fact, it never worked. "Parents help shape the world's future by the way they shape their children's values. The first step toward helping children live honorably is for parents to live a righteous life."[2] Our actions are copied by those closest to us. Our children are blank tapes, and we are filling their tape everyday. We have to be careful what we are giving them to record; they record only what they see adults do. We have to be careful what we download into our children. The question asked here is: "What kind of example are parents setting for their children?"

Children follow parent's example. In Genesis 26:7-11 there is a familiar passage that illustrates this point. Isaac was afraid that the men in Gerar would kill him to get his beautiful wife, Rebekah. So he lied, claiming that Rebekah was his sister. Where did he learn that trick? It is clear that he knew about the actions of his father Abraham, who many years earlier did the very same thing. (Gen 12:10-14 and 20:1-4).

Cain was born, and his name means "possession." Cain's mother had messed up, and his father had fallen. They desired a possession, a promise, a person that would restore them to their original paradise as God said one day her seed would. According to Genesis 3:15, God said to Eve, "And I will put enmity between you and the woman, and between your offspring and hers; he will crush your head, and you will strike his heel."[3] When Cain came forth, Eve projected her hopes and desires upon her boy. She knew he would be the one to get them back to paradise and destroy the works of the Evil One.

Our actions are copied by those closest to us.

The warning to all parents is that it is dangerous of parents to project upon their children what parents want them to be or need them to be. Too often parents want their children to become what they never became all in an effort to relive their lives through their children.

The examples of these displaced parental projections are too many to mention. In many cases parents never became the politician, so they are trying to make their children run for Mayor. The mother never became the head cheerleader, so she is trying to force her child into getting on the squad. The father never made it as a Billboard singer, so he presses his child to make the band. Parents will ruin their children with that errant psychological figure. Parents lived their lives, now the child must live his or hers.

If the story of Cain and Abel conveys nothing else, it demonstrates the obvious truth that children are going to make mistakes – and sometimes the mistakes they make are going to be huge! If parents haven't realized it yet, children aren't perfect. Our "little angels" often grow up to be "little devils" with rather large problems. Parents may want to act like their children are trouble free, but parents know that if given the space, their precious ones can turn into holy terrors without warning. Children will take the wrong road if you give them the wheel. Children will make mistakes because they've got some of us in them. Parents only hope that their children don't make the same mistakes they did.

Cain slew Abel, but maybe Cain's problem was that his momma smothered him and wouldn't let him grow up to be the man that God intended for him to be. The name Cain means "the possession." Eve was always running around talking about, "He's the one. He's the possession. That's my Cain. That's my possession." Every day of his life, every time he is called he is "the possession." When he was called for dinner, it was – "Time to eat Possession." When he was called for bed, it was – "Time to turn in Possession." When Cain was called for school, it was – "The bus is coming Possession." And then finally one day when he stands before God to make an offering, and he thinks that his offering will automatically be accepted because he has been told all of his life that "He's it; He's the one, He's the possession," and then he comes to discover that he's not "the One," such fury takes over his life. He's not "the One," and his world crumbles and anger fills Cain's life. Because all of Cain's life his mother pumped him up into believing he was something that he was not, when reality finally hits he is devastated.

His mother needs to cut the cord. Cain is still tied to his mother. She won't let him grow up and become a man. He was feeding off of his mother, and she kept obliging him. In order for boys to grow up to be men, mothers need to let them go.

He's not momma's little boy anymore. Some things little Billy has to learn to deal with on his own. Instead of calling momma to the school to fix it for Billy, at some point he's got walk into the Principal's office on his own. The real danger is being over protective, which will never allow him to grow into manhood. Too often little boys grow up weak and confused because they never got a chance to grow up. This developmental curse was illustrated in the movie *The Color Purple* when Sophia says to Mr. concerning his son Harpo: "Maybe he would have made somebody a decent husband if you would have let him grow up to be a man."

On the other hand, maybe Cain's problem was that his father didn't spend any time with him. He was trying to grow up on his own. His father was too busy running around outside of the Garden of Eden trying to figure out how to get back in. Perhaps Cain's father was too busy looking for paradise and forgot about spending time with his boy. Daddy Adam was too busy trying figure out where he went wrong. Cain's father was too lost in his own difficulties and didn't pay attention to what was going on with his own family. His father was too busy trying to make a living, killing weeds, and tilling ground for him to spend any time with his boys.

Fathers need to invest time in their children. When they are grown, parents don't get the time back. When those days are gone there is no rewind. In recent years, we speak of spending "Quality Time"[4] with our children, that time set aside specifically for the nurture of our children. However, our children not only need our quality time, they need our quantity time, our direct time, our indirect time, our talk time, and sometimes they just need for us to waste time with them.

In Ephesians 6:4, fathers are told to bring up their children in the nurture and admonition of the Lord. Admonition refers to the teaching part of training, and nurture refers to the disciplining part of it. Parents are to be an example, an encourager, and a restrainer.

The Ten Most Important Things To Say To A Child:
1. You are *Loved* – They need to know they are cared for.
2. You are *Important* – They need to know there is a place needed for them in the universe.
3. You are *Gifted* – They need to know they have something special to offer.
4. You are *Intelligent* – They need to know they can learn whatever they want to know.
5. You are *Wanted* – They need to know somebody appreciates them.
6. You are *Protected* – They need to know they are secure in the world.
7. You are *Growing* – They need to know where they are now is not where they are going to be.
8. You are *Needed* – They need to know what they bring to the table is essential to the development of the family.
9. You are a *Child of God* – They need to know there is a power greater than their own over their lives.
10. You are *Forgiven* – They will make mistakes and need to know when they make them, there is somebody there for them.

Fathers need to teach their boys how to be men. Just because they can fight, and impose their will upon another, does not mean they're grown. Just because a young man can make a baby doesn't make them a father, any more than standing in the garage makes one a car, holding a paint brush makes one an artist, putting a camera in one's hand makes one a photographer, or even putting a Bible under one's arm makes one a Christian. Discipline, responsibility, training, knowledge, internal composition, and personal accountability are some of the elements needed to carry such titles. Even so, manhood is about more than having the ability to make a baby. It is about fulfilling responsibilities, taking care of home, loving your wife, and providing for your children. It is about "dressing and keeping" your "garden."

I remind men everywhere that a man's first church is his home. Every man is called to be a pastor – the Pastor of his home. Every man is a Prophet, Priest, and King. That does not mean a man has all the answers or is right all the time, but it does mean he is willing to lead by example. As C. D. Williams has said, "You don't need to be right all the time. Your child wants a man for a father not a formula. He wants real parents, real people, capable of making mistakes without moping about it."

When fathers are the example and the godly inspiration in their homes, the rest of the family automatically comes closer to God. When a man's consistency of character and persistence in presence touches his family, it pleases God. It reminds me of the moving words of Quarles as he reflected on his father's example: "In early life I had nearly been betrayed into the principles of spiritual infidelity, but there was one argument in favor of Christianity that I could not refute, and that was the consistent character and example of my own father."

While fathers are teaching their sons to be men, mothers need to teach their girls how to be ladies. Mothers we need to teach our little girls to be ladies – not "floosies." Mothers need to teach their daughters that respect will come when they respect themselves. Wearing clothes that are so revealing does not gain respect. It may get a look, but it will never make a lady. To be treated like a lady, one has to act like a lady, and look like a lady, and speak like a lady.

Cain needed what every child needs: *Discipline* and *Direction*. The Bible says in Proverbs 22:6 "Train (that's discipline) up a child in the way (that's direction) he should go, and when he is old he shall not depart from it."

Children need *Discipline.* Children need to be trained. The need to train a child implies that he has a tendency to do what is wrong if left alone. Children want disciplined. They want to know that there is somebody that cares enough to correct them in love. The Bible says in Hebrews 12:6-11,

> For whom the Lord loveth he chastens, and scourges every son whom he receives. If ye endure chastening, God deals with you as with sons; for what son is he whom the father chastens not? But if ye be without chastisement, whereof all are partakers, then are ye bastards, and not sons. Furthermore we have had fathers of our flesh which corrected us, and we gave them reverence: shall we not much rather be in subjection unto the Father of spirits and live?...Now no chastening for the present seems to be joyous, but grievous: nevertheless afterward it yields the peaceable fruit of righteousness unto them which are exercised thereby.

Chastening repositions a child, gets them back in the right place. Where they may have gone astray, chastening redirects the errant behavior.

In fact, what happened to the day that children knew their place? What happened to the day when parents would be in the room having adult conversation, and one of the children would walk in and think they are going to hear what was being said and the parent would say, "This is grown folk talk. Get out of here!?" What happened to the day that dad could scold with a look, and mom could reprimand with a finger? Now the day has come when parents and children are watching the same thing, talking the same talk, and drinking the same drink.

There has to be a line of delineation between the parent and the child. Children get confused when they don't know who to check in with or to whom they are accountable. Keeping the parental boundaries is part of God's commandment to "honor your father and mother."

A person honors their father and mother, as Exodus 20:12 gives commandment, not just by bringing them flowers, and cooking them a meal, and getting them a card on their birthday or anniversary, but honor is given to a father and mother by staying out of trouble, living on the right side of the law, keeping your room clean, getting good grades in school, not using bad words, using your manners, making something of your life, working hard and staying out of jail.

Every child also needs *Direction* – someone to show them the way. No child should be left to develop by chance. Children are described in the scripture as "arrows." (Psalm 127:4) Arrows are the right analogy for children because arrows need directed. Arrows can be directed toward great evil (murder) or great good (defending lives). A child has great potential for either good or evil, depending on the type of training that he receives. What cannot be overlooked is that it is far easier to direct (train) a child because children are by nature more humble, pliant and trusting. Besides, bad habits have yet to be formed. Remember this: it is definitely easier to form than to reform. An important rule in training is that the earlier we train, the easier it is and the better the results (Proverbs 13:24).

The bottom line is using discipline and direction, every child needs somebody to support them, believe in them, and love them. After all, they are our future. They are the ones to whom this world will be left.

If parents are to raise healthy, positive, and God-fearing children, it would do parents well to embrace and post in our homes *The Children's Beatitudes*.

> Blessed is the child who has someone who believes in
>   him, to whom he can carry his problems unafraid.
> Blessed is the child who is allowed to pursue his
>   curiosity into every worthwhile field of information.
> Blessed is the child who has someone who understands
>   that childhood's griefs are real and call for
>   understanding and sympathy.
> Blessed is the child who has about him those who realize
>   his need of Christ as Savior and will lead him
>   patiently and prayerfully to the place of acceptance.
> Blessed is the child whose imagination has been turned
>   into channels of creative effort.
> Blessed is the child whose efforts to achieve have found
>   encouragement and kindly commendation.
> Blessed is the child who has learned freedom from
>   selfishness through responsibility and cooperation
>   with others.

Chapter VIII

Living Single

"When we are unable to find tranquility within ourselves, it is useless to seek it elsewhere."
— François de la Rochefoucauld

"My son, forget not my law; but let thine heart keep my commandments: For length of days, and long life, and peace, shall they add to thee."
— Proverbs 3:1-2

"My son, hear the instruction of thy father, and forsake not the law of thy mother: For they shall be an ornament of grace unto thy head, and chains about thy neck."
— Proverbs 1:8-9

My mother and father never experienced the "empty nest" because they didn't have a nest to empty. They had a bee hive, and none of their children were allowed to stay behind and suck up their honey. The "Queen Bee" told us early in our lives that all these little bees would have to get out soon and "make your own honey."

We moved out of the house quite early. Two had babies at seventeen, one got married at eighteen, another got married at twenty-two, one went to the military, and others moved on after college. I am not sure whether we were as glad to go as they were as glad to empty the hive. We approached the adult life for the most part inexperienced and with a level of naïvete that made us grow up in a hurry.

Moving out was difficult, but staying behind and getting stung with harsh words and even harsher looks was a fate too much for any inexperienced youngster to handle. Facing the big world had its advantages. We didn't have to hear my dad holler any more. We didn't have to be marshaled like outlaws any longer. We didn't have to take orders from our captain. We could do as we pleased and come and go when we wanted. But little did we know that facing the big world was also going to be extremely sobering and particularly frightening.

When I left the hive, I was married. I had gone to college at Boston University and later to the University of Pittsburgh, but I was still a long way from being ready for the real world. When I left, I was looking for a dissertation on "The Fine Art of Parenting" from my father. I was anticipating the lecture on "How To Treat A Woman" from my mother. I was waiting for the discussion on "Being A Man" from my father. I was looking forward to the "Philosophy of Leaving Home" from both of them. Instead, I got one unforgettable comment from my Dad when I told him I was getting married. He said, "That's your little red wagon…you've got to pull it."

For many maturing young adults, moving out and going it alone was much like a "Cain experience," an experience in meeting the world head on, wandering from place to place, and having to carry the weight of the world.

Cain was out in the world by himself. After he slew his brother Abel, God cursed Cain from the earth. In other words, he would no longer be able to be a farmer as he had been, but would be a wanderer from place to place, and would live from hand and to mouth. After Cain slew his brother, the Lord said to him, he shall be a "*fugitive* and a "*vagabond***,**" conveying the idea of wandering aimlessly.

Cain wanders from place to place as a lost man and gets to the land of Nod. He dwells in the land of Nod which literally is the place of "Wandering", a word with the same root as vagabond in Hebrew. Cain is out in the world wandering aimlessly like many who dare to leave "the hive" not knowing where he would go. Whether forced out or walked out, every young person who leaves home and is on their own has to determine a course of action.

The children's doctor, Dr. Seuss, was correct in his assessment of the way life will go. He said:

You have brains in your head.
You have feet in your shoes.
You can steer yourself in any direction you choose.
You're on your own.
And you know what you know.
You are the guy who'll decide where to go.[1]

Cain is removed from his home and from his family, and it will be his future decisions that will determine his final direction in life. No longer does he have his father to depend on. No longer does he have the luxury of eating his mother's home-cooked meals. No longer does he have his comfortable bed to sleep in and his favorite pillow to rest on. No longer is he afforded the conveniences of home. No longer is he able to pick up the phone and use it when he wants to. No longer can he go to the thermostat on the wall and turn up the heat. No longer is he able to look in the refrigerator and pull out a piece of bologna and fry it up in a pan, or get the peanut butter and jelly off the shelf and make a sandwich. No longer can he ask his dad for the car keys, and drive it till it's on empty.

Living single isn't easy! Every young person at some point in their life has to face the world on their own. They have to deal with leaving the place that was most comfortable for them and deal with a harsh, cruel, and vicious world. Inasmuch as every child wants to go out, and inasmuch as every parent wants their child to grow up and be on their own, it is still a difficult moment when it comes time to move out.

This chapter focuses on the Young Adults of the family, those who have moved beyond High School or College and will some day have a family of their own. This chapter addresses the group in the family that is about to venture out on their own, some going from place to place, and others landing careers and following their determined direction.

A quandary has developed for those in this category. They are in a most difficult yet most interesting place in life. They are the group that wants to be on their own but don't have all the resources available to do so: enough money saved, enough credit established, enough experience on their resume to move on with their life. The Young Adults is the group that is in between real adulthood and the responsibilities that come with it and the refreshing enjoyment of adolescence. They are the group that doesn't want to stay home, yet can't afford to move out.

This group is more likely of the late Busters Generation commonly called "Gen X'ers" that are very good at building and valuing strong relationships, while others are of the early Bridgers Generation that are often confident, ambitious, and community-oriented. They are the ones that will soon be married, soon have their own children, soon have their own homes, soon buy their own cars, and soon make their own family.

In fact, The Research Network on Transitions to Adulthood by the University of California – Irvine Department of Sociology suggests that there are Five Conventional "milestones" or "markers" in transitions to adult statuses:

(1) Not living with parents
(2) Not attending school
(3) Working full-time
(4) Married or ever married
(5) Has one or more children

The Research Network suggests that "these markers in transitions to adulthood are not as 'completed' or irreversible social accomplishments or changes in social status. Indeed, most (and arguably all) of the five are reversible, both in principle and in practice. So that, young adults who leave home at one point in time may return to live with their parents at a later age..."[2]

Children say they are grown while they are living at home, eating their parents' food, watching their parents' television, driving their parents' car, opening their parents' refrigerator, but the transition from young adulthood to adulthood doesn't really occur until they have moved out, are working, through school, married and with children.

It was what my father told his children when we thought we were grown: "As long as you are in my house, living under my roof, eating my food, enjoying my heat, sleeping in the bed I bought, wearing the clothes I purchased, watching the television I paid for, and paying no rent – you ain't grown yet! You might think you are but you just pretending."

I repeat, "Living Single" is a scary time of life for the young adult. Just as Cain thought his punishment too harsh for him, so do young adults who are transitioning into adulthood understand that this period of life can be a very intimidating time. In fact, Cain argues with God saying "my punishment is more than I can bear" to remind us perhaps that sometimes transitioning in life, going from "momma's to my own," just doesn't seem fair. It is an uncomfortable time, yet at the same time it is also an exciting time. You don't know whether you are going to make it or not. You are not sure how life is going to treat you. It's a great big world out there, and you have the excitement for living to go out and face the world but at the same time you have a reservation about it all to remain secure within your parental domain.

Perhaps this is the scariest time of your life because heretofore you have been taken care of by your parents, but now you will be parents and will wonder will you be able to provide for your own children. Heretofore you were a child and now you are thinking about having children. Heretofore you were the ones that kept every light on but now you will be faced with saying what was said to you, "Turn the lights out, we ain't got money to waste."

Isn't that crazy? Someday you will dread the thought of saying the things that your parents said to you that you promised yourself that you would never say to your children:

"I didn't ask who put it there, I said "pick it up!"

"Shut the door - I ain't trying to heat the whole neighborhood."

"Make sure you wear clean underwear, you might be in an accident."

"You don't want me to come back there."

"You better eat all your food; there are some kids in Africa that would love to have that."

"Shut up or I'll give you something to cry about."

"Don't you roll your eyes at me."

"Don't sit so close to the TV - you'll ruin your eyes."

"You will eat it and you will like it."

These are intimidating times for the young adult. These are the times that the young adult will wonder if their careers will pan out, if all of their college was worth it. They will be in suspense concerning their marriage, their transportation, their insurance, their health, their money, what they will eat, what they will wear, but I want them to know that they will make it. Young Adults will do well. They will prosper. They will have good success. Why? Because they are with God, and God is with them.

Even when Cain left home and became a vagabond, God still marked him as another act of God's grace and mercy toward him. It is best to take his mark as a personal sign for Cain, so that any that would try to avenge for the life of Cain's brother, God would guard. The message is clear, "As long as we do it God's way we get God's results."

Too often when we become old enough to move out we want to do it our way rather than God's way. We lose sight of God. We lose track of his goodness. We lose focus on what really matters. We lose the value of worship. We lose the commitment to church. We even lose the dignity in ourselves. As young adults getting ready to launch out on their own, my concern here is that in leaving home that you don't leave God.

There was an interesting study written in the magazine *Reconsider,* a Lifeway Biblical Solutions for Life publication. The article stated statistically that 70% of 23-30 year olds stopped attending church regularly for at least a year between ages 18-22.[3] The Young Adult drop-out rate in church was overwhelming. Now that momma can no longer make me go to church they stop attending. The publication suggests three main categories for the drop out: (1) Life changes or situations, (2) pastor related reasons, and (3) religious, ethical, or political beliefs. What's more is that the article goes on to report, "The Family is most instrumental in redirecting this trend. The importance of the religious practice and beliefs of parents and families cannot be overstated. From the study, several family-related factors contributed to young adults remaining in church, such as:

Parents still *married* to each other and both attending church when the young adult was 17.

Parents and family members *providing spiritual guidance*, praying together regularly, and actively serving in the church provides the avenue for sustained connection with God."[4]

One of the most important factors in dealing with the drop-out trend was *Fathers attending church* and parental expectations of church attendance. The biblical instruction in Deuteronomy 6:4-8 for parents to be the primary agents in the spiritual development of their children has not changed and should not be ignored. Parents must be encouraged and equipped to fulfill this important role and avoid the attitude that the church should be solely responsible for the spiritual instruction of their children.

My concern is that young adults, during this transition period, don't fall away from God.

The Church also has a key role in whether or not young adults stay plugged in to God after high school. A few of the church-

related factors that contributed to teenagers remaining
active in church include:
- Sermons relevant to their life as teenagers
- A worship style that was appealing
- A welcoming, non-judgmental environment
- Five or more adults making a significant investment in their
lives; personally and spiritually
- Having regular responsibilities at church[5]

The pressure is on for young adults because when one looks at
Cain, the successor of Adam, he has to make something of his life
that his daddy didn't make of his. Every young adult, while trying
to find their way, is at the same time expected to do more, be more,
know more, give more, serve better, than the generation before you.
Your parents will be proud of you regardless, but there is an
underlying clause that says: "You have to be more than what your
parents were" – even get closer to God than your parents did. I tell
my children that if you do not achieve more than I did, do more
than I did, love God more than I did, then I did something wrong.
As parent, my goal is to put something in my children that will take
them beyond where I went.

Yet, parents can't do it all. In order for their children to get
something out of life, the children have to want something in life.
Every maturing child has to want something, and want to be
something. It is still true, "whatsoever a man soweth, that shall he
also reap."(Galatians 6:7) Life won't be complete because a young
woman settles down with a young man, or because a young man finds a young woman to spend the rest of his life with. Sometimes what is discovered is that even when a person finds "the one," he or she will still,

Often relationships are built on the errant assumption that one person will make the other person better and happier.

at times, will appear to be a stranger. At times that person will act
like they don't know you and you don't know them suggesting that
life's satisfaction won't come because "somebody" is in your life.
The "complete" and "fulfilled" life will only come when there is a
connection with Jesus Christ. God is the fulfillment of life. Jesus

said, "I came that ye might have life and that ye might have it more abundantly."(John 10:10)

Now I talk about establishing young adult relationships. The first principle of note is: to get somebody that is about "something," i.e., someone that has direction, is focused, has drive, initiative, goals, ambition, good values, and productive behavior. The person seeking relationship has to also be about "something." Too many relationships are grounded in negative, non-productive foundations. Often relationships are built on the errant assumption that one person will make the other person better and happier. That's not true! The source of happiness and success only happens within you and that occurs as connection is made with God.

Every young adult needs to be careful not to enter into a relationship with someone that "ain't about nothing" just to say, "I have somebody." Those types of relationships are tragedies waiting to happen. They are relationships that offer nothing good for the pursuant or the pursued. They are called dead-end relationships – going nowhere and producing nothing but trouble. The old adage is true: "I can do bad all by myself."

Before a person settles down with someone else and attempts to make a lasting life-long relationship, first make sure you have settled yourself. Work on "you" first! Know what your goals are, know where you want to go, know what you want to be, know what you like, know what you don't like, know what that you're anchored. François de la Rochefoucauld said it this way: "When we are unable to find tranquility within ourselves, it is useless to seek it elsewhere."

The biggest problem with two people getting together is that two people get together and neither has a clue as to who they are. They spend most of their time in the relationship trying to figure each other out: what makes each other tick, who is in control, who has the power, and so on. The problem is not with the other person; it is with "you." Here is where we need to remember the words of Carl Jung, "Everything that irritates us about others can lead us to an understanding of ourselves."

A budding relationship should keep these tips in mind:
- Work on you first then you will appreciate the other person a little more. Most of the problems are not rooted in the other – they are in "M.E." My Engagements, My Excuses,

and My Ego. Don't assume there is something wrong with the other person – the problem might be with you.

- Listen carefully and give the other person the benefit of the doubt. Good communication skills will go a long way.
- Avoid blame. Do not point the finger at the other person.
- Create a "want-to" space. Make room for reconciliation in the relationship – a comeback point where the two can air out differences without losing individual dignity.

The taboo discussion yet remains, of which I now move quickly to its matter in this chapter. This is the discussion too often avoided by parents, anticipated by teenagers, and acclaimed by all. Nobody likes to talk about it, but it is definitely an engrossing family matter. The Hip-Hop stars of the 80's, *Salt 'N Pepa,* used to "rap": "Let's talk about *SEX* baby. Let's talk about you and me…"

Sex is not a topic that is easily discussed. Sex is one topic that too many parents want to avoid; however, if sex is not talked about, the youthful desires will go unchecked and uncontrolled.[6] Sex needs to be talked about in the home, in the family, and even in the church.

In fact, the Holy Bible has a lot to say about sex. Most importantly the Bible tells us that sex is good and is holy, but that is only if it is kept within the right boundaries. Hebrews 13:4 proclaims, "Marriage is honorable, in all, and the bed undefiled," which suggest that sex in marriage is the only acceptable place for such intimacy. If a person is in bed with someone, sexually intimate, and is not married, the bed is defiled. Defiled means polluted desecrated, dishonorable, corrupt, or ruined. Simply put, as one preacher has rightly said, "No Wed – No Bed!" The only honorable bed is the marriage bed because it is the true reflection of the covenant relationship between the man and the woman that represents the marriage covenant between God and His people.

Throughout the scripture God talks about His people in marital terms: how He is married to them; how He is jealous of them; how He loves them; how He is faithful to them. God designed marriage to represent his love between Himself and His people. When marriage does come for the young adult, follow the instruction of Ecclesiastes 9:9 and "Enjoy the wife of thy youth." Remember Proverbs 31:10 which says, "Who can find a virtuous

102

woman? For her price is far above rubics." And know Proverbs 18:22, "Whoso findeth a wife findeth a good thing, and obtaineth favor of the Lord."

In addition to the parameters for sex, the Bible also speaks of sexual "burning." I Corinthians 7:9 says simply, "It is better to marry than to burn." The burning here has several implications: to "burn with lust," to "burn with sexual desires," or to "burn with hell fires" to name a few. When sexual desires go unchecked and become out of control the flames of passion can consume all goodness within us. Marriage is God's way of "putting out the fire."

There is no such thing as "safe sex;" there is only "saved sex."

Parents need to be the first sex educators for their children. Please don't let HBO, MTV, or YouTube be the sex educator. Children are very impressionable and often think that what they see on television is true. Most of the time what they see on TV is not accurately relate in real life. Don't go by *Desperate Housewives*, and *Sex in the City*, and *The Game* because everyone of these contemporary television programs projects a relationship as nothing more than a commodity to be had at the others consumption and whoever becomes the "User" before they can be "Used" is the better. But A.I.D.S., and STD's, and other Venereal Diseases don't care who was the "used" and who was the "user." There's no such thing as "Safe Sex;" there is only "Saved Sex." There is only sex that has been ordained of, by, and through God.

Before the sex-talk, first let him treat you like a lady. Young ladies: don't give yourself away. Every generation needs to be reminded how to be "Ladies and Gentlemen." Here are some great tips for building respect in relationship:

Ladies:
1) Don't make him be less than a man with you. Let him treat you like a lady. If he doesn't he is not the one for you.
2) Have him come pick you up in his car – and have him open the door for you. You will discover it is the little things that make the difference.
3) Have him respect your home and your parents.
4) Let him show you how much he cares.

5) Never, never, never allow him to call you out of your name – you are not words reserved for dogs, and garden tools. If you respond, you will reduce to that level.

6) Have him pay for the meal – he should care enough about you to take care of the cost. Allow him to be a Giver.

Gentlemen:

1) Have her respect you not for what you have but for who you are. Character is always more important than cash. It is never what you have, but who you are that counts.

2) You make the first call. You be the pursuer.

3) Carry yourself like a man and let her appreciate you for your masculinity.

4) Pull your pants up – she will appreciate and respect you more for it. Let what you wear be a reflection of who you are.

5) Don't try to impress her with cash and clothes. Do it with character.

6) Hold on to your swagger. Your walk of confidence will say more than a thousand words.

Things have changed. It is no longer men seeking women for their pleasure, but the woman is now seeking the man. Too often women are doing for him trying to get the man, while he does nothing but sit and move from one woman to another. After he has gotten his fill of one, he moves on to stake his next claim.

"Living Single" isn't easy, but before the single person spends some time with someone else, first spend time with yourself. Every single person needs "Me-Time," that is time to get to know what you like and don't like, what you want and don't want. Jesus said, "Thou shalt love thy neighbor as thyself."(Matthew 22:39) The love of others starts with love of self and whether one remains single or anticipates a lifetime of marriage, the challenges still surface and a trust in God is essential.

Chapter IX

No Rocking Chairs For Me

"None are as old as those who have outlived enthusiasm."
                              – Henry David Thoreau

"They shall still bring forth fruit in old age; they shall be fat and flourishing."
                              – Psalm 92:14

O ur elderly are our treasure. They are our diamonds and pearls that have formed through long years of pressure and out of the depths of amazing resilience and lasting spirit. Having overcome countless obstacles, endless disappointments, and untold demands, these golden citizens are the shining spectacle that adds unimaginable value to family. Cherished, protected, and adored, these glorious relics are given highest regard and honor. After all, they possess the wisdom of the family. They provide for us direction. They give to us experience. They keep us grounded and remind us of what is most significant and most important in life. Having seen a few more sunrises and a few more sunsets, they have gained a greater perspective on life than those who have only lived past our formative years.

Heaven is only a few days away when the extended years surface. At this stage of life a reassessment occurs and life's finer features are explored. They already understand what my father said to me as I approached fifty, "Boy, you old enough now not to let your wants hurt you."

The elderly look at life through a different lens. They approach life with an uncommon outlook. Their cadence with God is different from the younger, unaccomplished, inexperienced person who is continually seeking the necessities of this world; whereas, the elderly are seeking the necessities of the world to come.

The elderly get up in the morning singing the spiritual, "Soon I will be done with the troubles of the world…goin' home to live with God." They go through their day with a greater appreciation for God's grace and goodness and are not concerned about what the day will bring but are focused on what awaits in heaven. They go to bed at night with a greater understanding of what it is to be blessed with another day. The elderly look at people through a lens of respect and dignity knowing that all life is a special gift from God. Older family members speak with words of inspiration and hope knowing that God's promises are sure, His leading is perfect, and His love is unmatched. They walk with the understanding that it will not be long till squeaky doors turn into pearly gates, and asphalt thoroughfares turn into golden streets, and worn out shoes turn into golden slippers, and tarnished goods turn into golden crowns.

As with all of our elderly, they did not have to earn their honor; they deserved it for simply the time they have put in and the number of their days. They spent their time investing in the lives of the young. The elderly gave us what they had received from life – for free. They handed to us the morality of the ages, the values of our ancestors, the wisdom of their experience, the guidance of years, and the truth of God. They showed us the way and gave us the light. And what we were commanded to give them was the unspoken rule of "Respect." As our beloved seniors, we automatically tipped our hat, nodded our head, and bowed at our waist. There was no talking back, no butting in, and no mean looks toward our elders. They were served first, confronted last, and held high.

We respected them because we knew all the "old timers" had value. Like old cheese that is best to taste, and old wine to drink, like old wood that is best to burn, old friends that are best to trust, old authors that are best to read, and old songs that are best to sing, growing old has its recompense.[1]

The "old timers" were my family's pride and joy. We had Granddaddy Lucian who stood as the preeminent patriarch of our family. In his late seventies, Granddaddy had more character amusements than Disney World in July. He was my father's father, and Granny's first of three husbands. Lucian, as he was more affectionately called, complained about the chronic pain that started in the nape of his neck, ran across his shoulder, down his back, and through his legs. For the everyday discomfort he would take a nip of Wild Turkey or Old Grand Dad that he would pull from their secret hiding places, to which, he would tell his mother, Victoria Nickens, with a slurred baritone voice, "Why momma, I ain't had a drink in years" – and she believed him.

We had "Cousin" Mary Francis who was close to ninety who lived in the back woods of Waterloo, Virginia and smoked a corncob pipe that she whittled out of a corn cob herself. To visit her, we had to walk through the path from our old house by the outhouse to get to her place that was an old log cabin of sorts. She would be sitting on her porch in a straw seat with her pipe clamped in her lips because she had no teeth saying, "Glad to see y'all. Don't nobody come see much."

Cousin Mary Francis was the lady that sold my parents one of her many acres of land for three hundred dollars. Because my parents couldn't afford it, Granny stepped in and purchased the land for them. They built a ranch style three bedroom home on that acre, and our family lived there four years before moving to Sewickley, Pennsylvania. Although I don't remember it, I was called "turd hopper" in Waterloo because once I had loaded my diaper, I would jump out of it and hop over its contents.

We had Aunt Rosie who was my mother's Great Aunt. She was a poor woman who took care of welfare children and when the children would get sick her cure was to wash them in dishwater and cabbage juice. She was a poor woman but was rich in warmth, will and welcome.

We had Victoria Nickens (Nannan), my father's grandmother, who was a neat, quick talking, fast acting half Soo Indian with straight black hair. She reminded me in stature, spirit and speech of "Granny" from *The Beverly Hillbillies*. Her father was a white man named John Wesley Grigsby from England who supposedly owned some sort of mill on the other side of town. My father said John Wesley Grigsby was called "Poppa." Nannan was the youngest of three sisters, and the three sisters were named after three Queens: Elizabeth, Isabel, and Victoria. Nannan's husband was William French "Buddy" Nickens, who was not the father of her son Lucian. Buddy's mother and Nannan's mother were sisters. Nannan lived

to be ninety-four years old.   We often contributed her long life
and abundant energy to her one-a-day vitamin the "King of Beers"
– a can of "Budweiser."

We also had Granny, Elveeta Slagle, a white woman that
lived in Warrenton, Virginia who was my father's mother. She had
one sister named Gladys, and Granny lived till she was sixty-nine.
She married three times, Lucian then Clark, and finally Bose. "The
Country" is what we called her place, and when we visited, ticks
were the final inspection of the children for the day. Granny would
make homemade ice-cream out of crushed ice, or, if it was winter,
from a fresh snowfall. Crisp scrapple, golden pancakes, scrambled
eggs, light biscuits, tender bacon, fried apples, and seasoned
sausage was the mouth-watering breakfast Granny made every
morning for us when we visited. She had chickens on her place,
and she would let us go into the chicken coop and get the fresh
eggs, and running the chickens was the sport of choice for all the
children. She was up before sunrise making breakfast, and soon
there was a feeding frenzy with thirty-four grandchildren waiting in
line for more. Carrot cake was her specialty. Everybody wanted
the last piece to take with them when we got back on the road. We
fought to be closest to her, but her love was big enough to embrace
us all.

Yet, the matriarch I remember most was my mother's mother,
Mary Julia Ball – Nanna. She was married twice, once to Charles
Nelson Tates, Sr., and then to John Gordon. When they divorced,
she never married again. Instead, she lived with us. She didn't
have a home of her own, so we would share her company during the
year. Half of the year she lived with us in Sewickley, Pennsylvania
and the other half she lived in North West, Washington, D.C. with
her son, Walter, his wife and six children. Rarely, she would visit
her other son, Uncle Junior (Charles Nelson Tates, Jr.) in Wichita,
Kansas. She also had three sisters that she would visit from time to
time: Aunt Margaret Jackson (Earl "Bunny" Jackson) who lived in
Virginia, and Aunt Sis, Harriet Jackson, who lived in Washington,
D. C., and Aunt Martha Campbell who lived in Warrenton,
Virginia.

Nanna didn't really care where she lived as long as she could
get to church. Her life was Jesus, all Jesus, and nothing but Jesus.
Church was her thing, and she dragged us to church whether we
wanted to go or not.   We didn't mind it much, but the
embarrassment came when we got there and she shouted. She was

the one that would talk back to the preacher during his message. She said she was just helping him preach. It was funny because none of the others assembled were helping. Then when the spirit hit her we ducked under the pew. Her "shout" got into the aisle, around the next pew, across the church, back down the aisle where she would usually end up laying out under the pew or falling out in somebody's lap. We were kids. What did we know about "getting the spirit?"

Besides church, Nanna had two other interests in her life. She had a green thumb and could grow anything. She would snap off a piece of a plant and root it in a glass of water. In a few days, she had a fully potted plant. She would talk to her ferns and her ivy like they could hear her.

Nanna was also the Black Betty Crocker. She could bake cookies fresher than Pillsbury. She made chocolate chip, chocolate chip with pecans, chocolate chip cookies with M&M's. Nanna made sugar cookies, sugar cookies shaped like stars, horses, reindeer, stars, bells, and Christmas trees. She made sugar cookies without sprinkles; she made sugar cookies with sprinkles – red sprinkles and silver sprinkles, and multi-colored sprinkles. She made peanut butter cookies, ginger bread cookies, snicker doodle cookies, Mexican cookies, lemon cookies, cherry cookies, butter cookies, cookies, cookies, and more cookies. She made tons of cookies then she put them in tin cans and gave them away to everybody in town.

We loved Nanna. She prayed for us, and she lived with us when she died at age sixty-five.

When Nanna died, we lived. I found life through her legacy of faith in God. The prayers she prayed became strength for us. As in every family, the legacy of our ancestors motivates the family's current members to greater achievement and renewed drive.

Now, the difficulty with these words on the aged is that I write from observation not from experience. Like Spurgeon, I too understand, "There is a blessedness about old age that we young men know nothing of."

Yet there is one profoundly obvious truth that I need not affirm: "If we live long enough, we all will get old." Time will carve crevices in our faces. Wrinkles will become etched on our brow. Our shiny locks will turn grey. Our knees will get weak. Our teeth will become few. And our eyes will grow dim. Solomon expressed this truth in Ecclesiastes chapter twelve reminding everyone that we don't stay young long, so enjoy it while you have it. One day we all will look around and twenty will be forty, and sixty will be seventy, and seventy will be one hundred.

Solomon reminds us that life is fragile and fleeting. Life is such a moment by moment experience. It is like "a silver cord [that's] loosed, or the golden bowl [that's] broken, or the pitcher [that's] broken at the fountain, or the wheel broken at the cistern." (Ecclesiastes 12:6)

To look at Solomon's words quickly, one possible conclusion is that getting old is unattractive. But to take a closer look at his description of aging and it is discovered that Solomon is telling us that the blessing to living is in remaining young at heart while the body grows old. Casey Stengel said the same when he mentioned the secret to old age is in "growing up without growing old." It was also what the century old comedian George Burns expressed when he said, "You can't help getting older, but you don't have to get old."

Getting old is in the mind. It is named in the heart. It is ascribed in the will. It is attached to the soul. Seventy, eighty, and ninety years do not prescribe old age. In fact, there are some very youthful eighty year olds. Solomon tells us to enjoy life while we've got it, regardless of age. In fact, it is what the Psalmist told us in Psalm 90:12, "Teach us to number our days that we may apply our hearts unto wisdom." Ashley Montagu had it right: "The idea is to die young as late as possible."

Senior citizens are our Wisdom. Why do you think God keeps them around? We are not to throw our aged away, and discard them like old clothes and old shoes. The aged are too often overlooked and treated like "has beens" – washed up, ineffective, unimportant and useless – nothing more than something to be set aside and discarded like expired produce that has rotted or dated milk that has spoiled.

Sons and daughters have a godly responsibility to care for their elderly. Western culture has primarily dismissed the notion of the family caring for its elderly. Our families tend to make the care of the aged somebody else's responsibility by sending them off to a senior facility – the "old folks' farm" where they are ultimately led out to pasture.

What happened to the day when grandma got old, or became widowed, and her children or grandchildren took her in? The bible says in James 1:27, "Pure religion and undefiled before God and the Father is this; to visit the fatherless and widows in their affliction." We are to take care of our older family members. Besides, the book of Titus 2:4-6 tells us that "the aged men and women are to teach the young men and women to be sober, to love their husbands, to love their children, to be discreet, chaste, keepers at home, good obedient to their own husbands, that the word of God be not blasphemed." The value of our seniors to teach and to train our young is indispensable. Seniors are a commodity we cannot afford to not cash in on. Old age routinely loses its value instead of gain in prominence.

In a sermon by Edward F. Markquart, he speaks of the impact of aging upon family and points out that, "In Leviticus 27, it is interesting to me that the value of a man's life is severely reduced when he crosses that invisible line of sixty years old. From ages 20-60, in Leviticus, a man's life is worth sixty shekels, but as soon as he turns sixty, his economic value drops to 15 shekels. His age crosses to sixty and his value drops four fold. Interesting! Modern America holds to similar views. When the senior line is crossed, the corporate world reduces the value. Corporate America has no use for the aged. It wants to retire them and move them out.[2]

What must be realized is that the fastest growing population in the world is with the aged. In America nearly forty million people are over sixty-five and our numbers are growing.[3]

Due to advanced medicine, more effective health care, better diet, sustained physical fitness, Americans are living longer. The fastest growing sector of the population is the hundred year olds. I know a 103 year old woman who is utterly amazing. At her age and with her Georgia blood, she is still fishing, still driving, still feeding her cows, still cooking at five o'clock every morning, still saving her money, still can tell a joke, still remembers what happened ninety years ago, still says what she will and what she will not do, still prays up a storm, and still worships the Lord.

Markquart, goes on to say, "We are aware that we are *living longer*, but we are not so aware that we are *living lonelier*," and suggests that "maybe our loneliness has to do with our increased mobility and the deterioration of our family relationships."[4] Sometimes we get around old people and we say, "They so mean." They are not mean; they may be lonely. They want somebody to see about them. They are not mean, they just want somebody that cares and is willing to check in on them from time to time.

The sad commentary on growing old is that we get over fifty or sixty years of age and the visitors become fewer. The sadder commentary on aging is that we begin to grow old and start talking about all of our regrets. What we never did! The dreams we never fulfilled. The places we never went. The dances we never danced. The vacations we never took. The people we never thanked. We start focusing on all of the "Could-a, Would-a, Should-a's" that hold us back from living the rest of our lives. Fewer visits are one thing, but when hopes and dreams stop showing up that's fatal. "A man is not old," as John Barrymore explained, "until regrets take the place of dreams."

As this chapter is read, there is one compelling question that should be answered: "What is your dream? What is it at seventy-three or eighty-three that you are still looking forward to?" "A man is not old," says Jean Rostand, "as long as he is seeking something." Likewise, Henry David Thoreau said, "None are so old as those who have outlived enthusiasm."

Never stop dreaming! When enthusiasm has departed and motivation has vanished, death has already arrived. Some people died twenty years ago – they just have not been buried yet. They died when the business went under, when the divorce became final, when the children all left home, when the loan was denied, when the money ran out, or when the investments fell through. More than counting up our years, we need to make our years count!

Quit talking about age. Age is a number. You are as young as you feel. Seventy-five is only a number. At seventy-five, we are, as is commonly reported, really thirty with forty-five years experience. The problem with getting old is we start to act like it. We think old, talk old, walk old, and act old. You can if you want to, maybe not as fast, or as high, or as long as before, but you still have it in you to live.

> Some people died twenty years ago – they just aren't buried yet.

Many spokespersons on aging have reminded us that age is only a number. Samuel Ullman, for example, declared, "Nobody grows old merely by living a number of years. We grow old by deserting our ideals. Years may wrinkle the skin, but to give up enthusiasm wrinkles the soul." Douglas MacArthur stated, "You are as young as your faith, as old as your doubt; as young as your self-confidence, as old as your fear; as young as your hope, as old

as your despair." And Oliver Wendell Holmes affirmed,
"Men do not quit playing because they grow old; they grow old
because they quit playing."

Rocking chairs will not be for me – I will prefer a sled. In
thirty years from now, when I am touching eighty, I want to take to
the slopes and dash my way down a snow-covered hill with the
wind whistling across my face and the glide of the blades swishing
beneath me, with my cheeks red from the winter cold. That is
living!

Here are seven tips on "How to Stay Young":

1. **LEARN** – *Keep learning.* You can still learn
   something about what you already know or you can
   learn something new. Keep your mind active.
2. **LIST** – *Make a "Bucket List."* Ask yourself, "What
   would I like to do before I die?" – Then do it! You
   still have time.
3. **LOOK** – *Enjoy the simple things.* Appreciate the
   flowers that grow in the garden and the cows as you
   see as you ride along the highway. You will be
   surprised at what you will see and the things you've
   never noticed, yet they have always been there.
4. **LAUGH** – *Laugh often, long and loud.* Laugh at
   anything and everything. You have taken life
   seriously enough.
5. **LIVE** – *You will die soon enough.* Live every day
   like it is your last – some day you will be right.
6. **LOUNGE** – *Kick back with the people, you enjoy
   most,* whether it's family, or friends. Sip on cold
   lemonades in the summer time and make sure you
   taste the lemon.
7. **LOVE** – *Love everybody.* Tell those that mean the
   most to you that you love them as often as possible.

"When it comes to staying young," Marty Bucella proclaimed
that "a mind-lift beats a face-lift any day." As we grow older, the
blessedness and beauty of life moves from the externals to the
internals. We get old because as McQuilkin explains, "God has
planned the strength and beauty of youth to be physical. But the
strength and beauty of age is spiritual. We gradually lose the

strength and beauty that is temporary, so we'll be sure to concentrate on the strength and beauty which is forever."⁵ Martin Buxbaum was right: "Some people, no matter how old they get, never lose their beauty – they merely move it from their faces into their hearts."

The prophet Joel said, "Old men shall dream dreams, your young men shall see visions." The truth is at seventy, eighty, ninety, or one hundred, there is still a lot of life and a lot left to contribute to the world.

At 80 Moses received his call to tell Pharaoh to "Let my people go."

At 80 Caleb went up to war.

At 90 and 100 Sarah and Abraham received the child of promise.

At 89 Michelangelo was still producing masterpieces.

At 80 Verdi was still writing operas.

At 70 Kant wrote some of his greatest philosophical work.

At 83 Gladstone served as Prime Minister of Germany.

At 69 Ronald Reagan became our nation's oldest elected president.

At 100 George Burns was still telling jokes.

At 75 John Glenn returned to space.

At 95 Bob Hope was still performing.

At 63 Mike Melvill landed SpaceShipOne after becoming the first private pilot to earn astronaut wings.

At 70 George Brunstad was the oldest person to swim the English Channel.

At 78, Bill Anderson started his quest to Bicycle across the nation both ways.

At 90 my great-grandmother, Victoria Nickens, took her first motorcycle ride on the back of my father's 750 Honda.

At 70 my mother announced her call to the ministry and was licensed to preach the Gospel of Jesus Christ at age 72.

At 75 my father is still the Pastor of the Love Hope Baptist Church.

Charles Lamb said it well: "We grow gray in our spirit long before we grow gray in our hair." We get old, and all the world is yet before us. No matter how old we are, no one can stop us from making our contribution to the world, having a positive attitude about life, and living with continued grace and grandeur.

Chapter X

ALL IN THE FAMILY

"In every conceivable manner, the family is link to our past, bridge to our future."
                                        -- Alex Haley

"...Who is my mother? And who are my brethren?...For whosoever shall do the will of my Father which is in heaven, the same is my brother, and sister, and mother."
                                        – Matthew 12:48, 50

P utting down the *T.V. Guide*, my family and I picked up our Bibles. Who would have believed it? – that the Grigsby's, who were as far removed from God as the next heathen clan, could enter the saving knowledge of God and become a brigade of bold believers for Christ Jesus. Ghostly families don't become godly neither do hellish ones become holy, except the power of God take over them.

Becoming a part of the church and working for God was the furthest thing from our minds. We were too busy enjoying the motorcycle rides on Sundays, the Steeler games on Sunday afternoons, and Sunday softball on Chadwick Street. We didn't have time for God. Yet, the unusual thing is that God had time for us.

We were moved from a family of maniacs to a family on a mission for God. One by one we were summoned of God to carry the Gospel forth to the world, to edify His people, and to encourage

116

those who were brokenhearted. Our lives would be forever changed.

My grandmother had proclaimed, as she observed our untoward home life, "I might not live to see it, but one day God will save us all." The year Nanna died God started a great transformation with our family.

My brother said, when I mentioned to him that we were borderline dysfunctional, "We were not borderline, we crossed the line and came back." Our coming back was not by our own devices, but the power of God converted us from a family of perpetual problems into a family of passionate preachers.

I was called to preach the Gospel of Jesus Christ in September, 1980 and was licensed to preach one month later. Five years after that I was called to Pastor in Ford City, Pennsylvania. After serving along the Allegheny River for ten years, God planted me in the city of Pittsburgh at the historical Central Baptist Church, and I became the ninth Pastor in their one hundred nineteen year history. I have been privileged to serve there almost fourteen years.

In less than a year after my call to preach, my brother Canard was called to preach and licensed and would eventually go on to Pastor the First Baptist Church in Bridgeville, Pennsylvania and then the Morningstar Baptist Church in Clairton, Pennsylvania.

As God ordained, in November 1979 my father went from a professor of profanity to a preacher of the Gospel and then was licensed in November 1982. He has been the Pastor of the Love Hope Baptist Church in Ellwood City, Pennsylvania for twenty-seven years.

Not to be excluded from God's ministerial sweep through our home, my mother was called to preach in 2004 and was licensed to preach the Gospel of Jesus Christ in October 2006.

My sister Elizabeth married a preacher, and my sister Elaine serves as a Deaconess at the Calvary Baptist Church in Baltimore, Maryland. My sister Doris rededicated her life to the Lord after a debilitating stroke. And my oldest brother Walter is most inquisitive about the things of God and is more biblically and theologically astute than most, yet he claims to be an inquiring agnostic.

As I have taken the time to reflect upon my ancestry in recent months, God's intervention in our family is much clearer to me now. Going back to my great-great-grandfather, John Wesley Grigsby – "Poppa", it is clear to see how our family was destined to be God's servants. "Poppa" was named after one of England's greatest eighteenth century theologians, John Wesley. John Wesley, born 1703, was an Anglican cleric and Christian theologian. Wesley started a movement of practical piety. This concern for holiness of heart and life led Wesley to create specific "methods" of Christian living. Thus, John Wesley founded the English Methodist movement, Methodism, which began when he took to open-air preaching. John Wesley's brother, Charles Wesley, was also a great 18th century theologian and wrote some the churches greatest hymns.

As I see my place in ministry and understand my call of God now, my family and I are fulfilling the ancestral plan for our family. We were named after the name, John Wesley, who was marked to touch the world for God, and I believe that mark, that call, has been placed upon us. Our ancestral destiny is being fulfilled.

In a strange way, I couldn't have done anything else with my life. I was destined by God and determined by ancestral call to preach the Gospel to all people. No wonder my Mechanical Engineering degree was overridden, and my philosophical and theological thirst became so pronounced. I was called to preach the Gospel and had very little to do with it. Sure, I had a choice, but the ancestral prayers of the past positioned our home for and helped shape our destiny. Like so many families who have, for generations, occupied the same profession, occupation, or career, there is in every family an ancestral link to the past that shapes our present and bolsters our future.

We are a family of preachers. We didn't start out that way, but the power of God to transform lives and families is real. The evidence speaks for itself. God can do anything, with anybody, at anytime, and in any home. In spite of all the rocky moments, my father and mother have been married for fifty-two years. They have been in pastoral ministry for twenty-seven years and have brought countless souls to the Lord. Their faithfulness in marriage and in ministry has been sustained only by the power of God and has led to the continual call of God upon their children and their childrens' children.

Nanna's words were true. Somehow she knew that God would do something extraordinary with our family, and there is a sense in which, with all that has already been done, God has only just begun to reveal the greater works that yet remain for the next generation.

God is moving again in our home and has begun to call a next generation of Christ's servants to preach the Gospel and labor for the Kingdom. As the next generation of believers in our family arises, God again is making a clean sweep in our homes with my children, my nieces, and my nephews.

My wife and children are servants of the Most High God. All of my children have surrendered their lives to the will of God. Their call is to bring the families of men to a stronger place as the families of God. We have been given the awesome mandate of God to spread the love and the Word of God. We have committed to closing racial divides, crossing economic boundaries and continually preaching the Gospel so that all people might be brought into the saving knowledge of Jesus Christ as the family of God.

In fact, it was my grandmother who taught me that the family of God is bigger than the family of man. Nanna was born in 1911 and died in 1977. She had three sisters and no brothers. One of her sisters was Aunt Margaret, another we called Aunt Sis, Harriet was her real name, and the other was Aunt Martha Campbell.

I was very young, around eight years old, when I learned of these wonderful matriarchs who were really a special part of our family. We cherished them. Nanna was a holy woman. She never missed church, prayed without ceasing, read her Bible every day, shouted unashamedly, and gave anything she had to anybody. I never heard her sware. I never heard her say anything mean to anybody. I was named after my Grandmother, Nanna. In fact, I was named after two of the matriarchs of our family. Nanna's name was Mary Julia, and my middle name, Julius, was after her. I was also named after my great grandmother, Nannan. Her name was Victoria Nickens. My name is Victor Julius Grigsby.

Nanna only had three sisters, yet she referred to all the women in her circle as her "sister" – Sister Bell, and Sister Mary, and Sister Bertha. She had no brothers, yet to all the men in her company she referred to them as her "brother" – Brother Bill, Brother Thomas, and Brother Smith.

I was confused. I went to my mother and asked with an eight year old's curiosity, "Where Nanna get all these brothers and sisters?" My mother said, "Nanna belongs to the biggest family in the world. Her brothers and sisters are 'all in the family' – the family of God."

What my mother said to me was what Jesus was saying to his disciples when he was in the house teaching. This revolutionary teaching is recorded in Matthew 12:46-50, again in Mark 3:31-35, and again in Luke 8:19-21. The room was packed. Nobody else could get in the house. I imagine people were standing around the walls and seated in the window sills. Jesus was teaching to a packed house when Jesus' mother, brother, and sister showed up at the door. It was so crowded that they couldn't get in the house. One of the disciples pulled over close to Jesus, looked at Him and said, "Ah, Jesus! Your people are at the door. What you gone do? Want me to tell some of these folk to back up so they can get in?"

Jesus looked around at the scene, saw people in front of him that were feeding on the word of God, looked behind him and noticed people in worship posture, looked beside him and saw people who had sacrificed everything to follow him, looked all around him and saw people who were walking in obedience to God and said to his disciples, "Who is my mother, my brother, or my sister?"

It seemed to be a strange response from the Messiah. It seemed like a strange response coming from the man who had some time ago been teaching on the Commandments and said, "Thou shalt Honor your father and your mother." It seemed like a very unusual reply considering he was the one that suggested that "a house divided against itself cannot stand." and taught us saying, "let a man leave his father and mother and cleave unto his wife," and "what God has joined together let no man divide asunder." It seemed to be a strange response considering that Jesus was "pro-family," yet Jesus wasn't being disrespectful or dishonorable concerning his family. He was making a point: *spiritual* connections run deeper than *physical* ones.

In this short scene, Jesus was long on spiritual relationships. There is little comparison between earthen relationships to those relationships born out of heaven. The *Life Application Bible* explains: "Spiritual relationships are as binding as physical ones, and he was paving the way for a new community of believers –the universal church – our spiritual family."[1] What is most important to note is that physical connections are temporary, but spiritual relationships are eternal.

The comments on Matthew 12:46-50 in the *Nelson Study Bible* are also striking:

Jesus called attention away from earthly relationships to more important spiritual relationships. His words were not intended to be one of disrespect to Mary or to His brothers, for they too would come to share the spiritual relationship. However, there is no suggestion here at all that Jesus' mother had any special access to His presence or any particular influence over Him. By using this startling question, Jesus prepared the crowd to receive the precious truth that whosoever shall do the will of his Father was, in fact, His mother, His brother, and His sister."[2]

Jesus was letting us know that there was an earthly family and that there is the family of God. Jesus makes it perfectly clear that although we may live in the same house, we have greater connection when we are connected to the house of God. Although we may have been carried in the same womb, we have greater connection when we worship the same God. Although we may live at the same address, we have closer connection when we have accepted the Lord as Savior.

Family is family once because of genetic descriptions, but family is family twice because of Jesus declarations. In Christ Jesus, we are linked together in family by the invisible thread of God's presence that abides in our hearts and souls. When we are born once by the same mother, we are connected physically – earthly relationship; when we are born again by the same Spirit, we are connected spiritually – heavenly relationship.

In John 1:11-12: "He came to his own and his own received him not, but to as many as received him to them gave he the power to become the sons of God." When we receive Jesus Christ into our lives and acknowledge Him as our Lord and Savior, we become a part of God's family. He gave us the power and privilege to become a part of the family. Being in God's family comes down to this song of worship:

It's the Jesus in you that loves the Jesus in me;
And the Jesus in me, loves the Jesus in you.
So easy, easy to love.

The connection that God has given between every believer is described in what I call "Barney Theology," the big purple dinosaur's theme song:
I love you. You love me.

We're a happy family,
With a great big hug and a kiss from me to you.
Won't you say you love me too?

It's a matter of the heart that makes one a part of the family of God. It is not by external features that we are associated with one another spiritually. It is by the internal composition of the heart that we are family. Just as we are family because of our internal DNA, we are the family of God because of our spiritual DNA.

Physical descriptions do not place us in the family of God. We are in the family of God because of our spiritual features. Romans 2:28-29 says, "For he is not a Jew, which is one *outwardly*; neither is that circumcision, which is outward in the flesh: But he is a Jew, which is one *inwardly*; and circumcision is that of the heart, in the spirit, and not in the letter; whose praise is not of men, but of God." The *Life Application Bible* comments: "To be a Jew meant you were in God's family, an heir to all his promises. Yet Paul made it clear that membership in God's family is based on internal, not external qualities. All whose hearts are right with God are real Jews – that is, part of God's family."[3] Attending church has little to do with you being in the family. Being baptized is of little consequence. Being accepted for membership and on the church roll is not enough. Just as circumcision was not enough for the Jews. What God wants from us is our faithfulness, devotion and obedience.

Ephesians 3:14-15 tells us "For this cause I bow my knees unto the Father of our Lord Jesus Christ, Of whom the whole family in heaven and earth is named." The *Life Application Bible* suggests, "The great family of God includes all who have believed in him in the past, all who believe in the present, and all who will believe in the future."[4] We are 'All In The Family' because we have the same Father. He is the source of all creation, the rightful owner of everything. God promises his love and power to his family, the church; if we want to receive his blessings. It is important that we stay in contact with other believers in the body of Christ. "Those who isolate themselves from God's family and try to go it alone are cutting themselves off from God's power."[5]

My brother and I are family twice – once because we have the same mother and father, but twice because we are brothers again by the new life we have received in Christ Jesus. Anybody that has new life in Christ is also my brother and my sister bound together in a loving, peaceful, harmonious spiritual relationship. We are fighting our own people, those who are in the family. We are not battling the enemy, but unfortunately there are brothers fighting brothers and sisters fighting sisters. How strange it is that if one would not talk about their natural brother, why would they talk about their spiritual brother? If one would not hurt their natural brother, why would they hurt their spiritual brother? If one would not offend their natural brother, why would they offend their spiritual brother?

There is a song of the church descriptive of the bonds between believers in Christ:

I need you, you need me.
We're all a part of God's body.
Stand with me. Agree with me.
I need you to survive.
I pray for you, you pray for me.
I won't harm you with words from my mouth.
I need you to survive.

Jesus' words in Mark 3:31-35 suggests that God's family is open and doesn't exclude anyone. Although Jesus cared for his mother and brothers, he also cared for all those who loved him. Jesus did not show partiality; he allowed everyone the privilege of obeying God and becoming part of his family. He shows us how to relate to other believers that are now apart of the new community in faith. That's significant because in our increasingly computerized, impersonal world, warm relationships among members of God's family take on major importance.

Remember before Alexander Graham Bell invented the telegraph when someone wanted to borrow a cup of sugar from their neighbor, they had to get up, go next door, make a personal appeal, speak to their neighbor and ask for the sugar? Then with the telephone, they didn't have to see anybody. A person just got on the phone and said, "May I borrow a cup of sugar? Yeah, just leave it on the porch I will get it." And now the imperonsalization from neighbor to neighbor has increased to the point where a person doesn't have to see them or speak to them, one just leaves a text message and says, "Need Sugar...Borrow some...your neighbor. TAL(thanks a lot)." We have become such an impersonal culture, but the church can give loving, personalized care that a person can't find anywhere else.

Luke 8:21 reminds us that "Jesus' true family are those who hear and obey his words. Hearing without obeying is not enough. As Jesus loved his mother, so he loves us. He offers us an intimate family relationship with him."[6] Jesus said, "Who is my mother, my brother, my sister, but those who will do the will of God."

We are the Family of God, but it is interesting to note that God only chooses those to be in it that are not His. God had only one "begotten" Son, all others in the family are adopted in. Those who are in God's family are those who didn't belong to there. God chose them. According to Ephesians 1:5, "Having predestinated us unto the adoption of children by Jesus Christ to himself, according to the good pleasure of his will," we have become a part of the family of God. Galatians 4:5-7 says, "That we might receive the *adoption* of sons. And because ye are sons, God hath sent forth the Spirit of his Son into your hearts, crying, Abba, Father. Wherefore thou art no more a servant, but a son; and if a son, then an heir of God through Christ." Those who are in the family of God are those who have been adopted in, brought in not because we deserved to be there but because we were by grace made a part.

Our families are intended to represent God's family. We are to "Re–Present" God's family. When someone sees a family they are to see the family of God. Families are to reflect the qualities, the characteristics, the traits, the very nature of God: His love, His goodness, His mercy, His kindness, His joy, His peace, His forgiveness, His compassion, His grace. When we see an unforgiving, unloving, unkind, merciless, ungracious family, we have to wonder where is God in the family?

Does that mean our family is perfect? Again, resoundingly – No! It means that we understand what grace is. It means we understand what mercy is all about. It means we understand what it means to forgive and be forgiven. It means we understand what Love is. It means we understand what redemption is about. Never think your family is perfect or has to be perfect. It is not. Every family has its problems.

One of my regularly viewed television shows I will not forget: *The Munsters*. It was the crazy looking family that came on everyday after school at about 4:30. I loved to watch *The Munsters*: Herman with the bolts out of the side of his neck, Grandpa hanging upside down in the basement like a bat, Lily dressed in coffin attire, the boy Eddie who had fangs, Spot the fire breathing dragon that stayed under the steps, and Marilyn the supposedly odd-ball fashion model in the family. They were a strange, abnormal, and somewhat frightening bunch of which everyone who entered their home or came in their presence thought them to be quite scary.

The message from *The Munsters* was clear to me: Family can be the most unusual, most outrageous, most unpredictable, and often frightening thing, but as long as those in the family love and appreciate each other, it doesn't matter what the outside world says or thinks about them; it doesn't matter how family looks to the outside world as long as they have love and respect for one another. Never mind what everybody else says about "You and Yours," it may look pretty scary to outsiders, but if those within it understand it, and appreciate it, then it is all good. Even with dragons hidden under the steps, it's how you deal with what's under there that counts.

Beyond the silver, and gold, and cars, and land, and diamonds, one of God's greatest resources is family. Proverbs 11:29 tells us, "He that troubleth his own house shall inherit the wind." The implication in this scripture is that "One of the greatest resources God gives us in the family. The family provides acceptance, encouragement, exhortation, and counsel. Rejecting ones' family – whether through anger or through an exaggerated desire for independence – is foolish because you cut yourself off from all they provide. We strive in our families for healing, communication, and understanding."[7]

A person shouldn't have to look anywhere else to find the love they need – the family is the place that provides it. One shouldn't have to look outside the home for support, protection, motivation, or encouragement – it's all in the family. One should be able to look in their family and the family of God for all they need to make it in life. George Moore said, "A man travels the world over in search of what he needs, and returns home to find it."

Over the arch of every home should be placed the words of the Psalm:
Blessed is every one that feareth the Lord;
that walketh in his ways.
For thou shalt eat the labour of thine hands:
happy shalt thou be, and it shall be well with thee.
Thy wife shall be as a fruitful vine by the sides of
thine house: thy children like olive plants round

about thy table.
Behold, that thus shall the man be blessed that
feareth the Lord.
The Lord shall bless thee out of Zion; and thou
shalt see the good of Jerusalem all the days of
thy life.
Yea, thou shalt see thy children's children, and
peace upon Israel. – Psalm 128

A good family life is a reward for following God. Our comforts, our joys, and our services are established from our homes, and a good place to start to make every family all it can be is with reading and obeying God's Word.

As for me, I spend most of my time these days with John, Paul, Mark, James, Jude, Luke, and Matthew. My time with my former acquaintances have become less and less. Jay Jay, Lamont, Greg, "Meathead" and the "Beave," have become a thing of the past, and as I fold my hands at night and close my eyes, the sounds of "Good Night" echoing through our home have quieted. My anticipation now is not in the recurring calls of "Good Night, John Boy" but in the refreshing sighs of, "Good Morning, Jesus."

Appendix A

Our

Family Covenant

BELIEVING THAT GOD, IN HIS WISDOM AND PROVIDENCE,

has established our family in covenant relationships and as a sacred and lifelong commitment, expressing our unconditional love for one another and believing that God intends for our family to carry out the commission of Jesus Christ as witnesses of the gospel,

We do hereby affirm our solemn pledge to fulfill our Christian values, our Biblical beliefs, and our abiding love through Jesus Christ our Lord.

Furthermore, we pledge to exalt the blessed nature and permanence of our family covenant by calling others to honor our family vows.

In The Presence of God

And these witnesses, and by a Holy covenant, I, the man of God, prayerfully vow before God to protect, provide, and care for my family. I vow to honor my wife and raise my children in the fear and admonition of the Lord. I recognize I am the priest, prophet and king of my home and promise to walk in obedience to the Spirit of God. I will remain prayerful over my family, loyal to my church, and faithful to my God.

In The Presence of God

And these witnesses, and by a Holy covenant, I, the woman of God, prayerfully vow before God to respect my husband as the head of the family. I promise to nurture and comfort my

children teaching them to acknowledge God in all
their ways. I vow to support my husband, encourage my
children and love my   family. I am the queen of my home and
the backbone of my family. I solemnly vow to speak truth in
love and remain virtuous in character. I vow to be steadfast,
faithful and ever true to my God.

In The Presence of God

And these witnesses, and by a Holy covenant, I, the child of
God, prayerfully vow before God to honor my parents. I
promise to respect, love and obey my parents as God has
ordained. I promise to live before God a holy and righteous
life and seek those things which are of God. I am "fearfully
and wonderfully made." I am an original masterpiece. I vow
to walk with integrity, stand in humility, and live in harmony
with God and my family.

In The Presence of God

And these witnesses, and by a Holy covenant, I, the Senior of
God, prayerfully vow before God to live an exemplary life
before my children and grandchildren. I promise to teach my
family the ways of God and share with them the wisdom that
God has given me. I vow to be a testimony of faith and a
symbol of righteousness. I will remain a pillar for my family,
a guide for my church and a worshipper of my God.

In The Presence of God

And these witnesses, and by a Holy covenant, we, the family
of God, prayerfully vow before God to love, laugh and live
together in the presence of God. We promise to forgive each
other in moments of wrong, comfort each other in moments of
sorrow, trust each other in moments of trial, and pray for each
other continually. We vow to stay together as a family so that
we will live together eternally as the family of God.

130

_____   _____
Father's Signature   Mother's Signature

_____   _____
Child's Signature   Child's Signature

_____   _____
Child's Signature   Child's Signature

_____   _____
Child's Signature   Child's Signature

_____
Grandparent's Signature

_____
Grandparent's Signature

_____
Grandparent's Signature

_____
Grandparent's Signature

Appendix B

132

Walter,	Doris,	Elaine,	Canard, Jr.,	Elizabeth,	Victor
(Rocket,	Mouse,	Boo,	Corkie,	Issy,	Jay)
7-2-52	2-26-54	12-31-58	5-18-59	9-5-60	9-1-61

(Back Row l-r) Elaine, Walter, Doris
(Front Row l-r) Victor, Elizabeth, Canard, Jr.

Victor,   Elizabeth,   Elaine, Doris,   Walter,   Canard, Jr.

Thelma Virginia Grigsby (b. April 27, 1933)
(My Mother: pic.September 26, 1972)

My Mother – June 1958

My Mother – 4 years old
(pic. October 5, 1937)

My Mother – 17 Years old – (pic. 1950)

134

Canard S. Grigsby, Sr. (b. November 11, 1934)
(My Father)

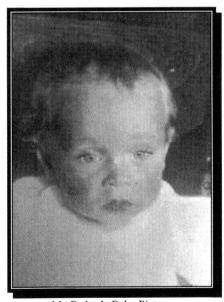

My Father's Baby Picture

135

Canard S. Grigsby, Sr.
(My Father: 1952 Jamaica, NY)

My Father standing at the 3/8 pole in Jamaica, NY 1952
(The Jamaica Race Track)

Canard, Michael, William, Elveta (Peggy), **Lloyd, Leon, John**
My Father and his brothers and sisten

My Father

My Mother

My Father and Mother: Married
Dec. 22, 1956

My Mother and Father:
52 Years of Marriage

Elveta Slagle Grigsby – (Granny)
(b. February 19, 1910 – d. 1979)

Granny and her sister Gladys

My Father and His Mother (Granny)

138

Mary Julia Ball – (Nanna)
(b. August 13, 1911 – d. 1977)

Charles Nelson Tates, Sr. & Mary Julia Tates

My Father and Nanna

Aunt Rosie Thompson
(Nanna's Aunt)

Aunt Margaret Jackson
(Earl "Bunny" Jackson)
(Nanna's Sister)

Aunt Sis – Harriet Jackson
(Willie Jackson)
(Nanna's Sister)

Aunt Martha Campbell (Her Child)
(Nanna's Half Sister)

Uncle Junior (Rita), **Uncle Walter** (Vivian)

Uncle Walter, Aunt Vivian
Tawana, LeEtta, Walter, Jr., Linda, Clayton, Buddy

141

John Lucian Grigsby – (Granddaddy)
(b. January 5,1909 d. July 31, 1988)

Granddaddy

Molly Victoria Grigsby-Nickens
(Nannan July 29, 1888 – December 19, 1982)

Nannan – Her Younger Years

Nannan and her father John Wesley Grigsby

Nannan

Isabel Grigsby
(Victoria's Sister)

John Wesley Grigsby "Poppa"[b. 1846(circa) – d. 1936]
(Nannan's Father)

John Wesley Grigsby – "Poppa"
(My great-great-grandfather)

144

Victoria, Lucian, Canard, Elizabeth, Amica
(Five Generations)

Nannan, Leon, Canard, Sr.

Cousin Mary Francis

Cousin Mary Francis' Pipe

Cousin Mary Francis

Cousin Mary Francis' Hand-Carved Corn-Cob Pipe

Adolfus Smoot & Mary Francis Lawson Bailey Smoot

Cousins

147

First Row(l-r): Elaine, LeEtta, Tawana, Linda, Walter, Jr.
Second Row(l-r): Canard, Jr., Elizabeth, Victor

(l-r)**Tawana, Elaine, Linda, Elizabeth, Victor**

**Uncle Leon, Lecia, Elaine, Leon, Jr.,
Steve, Canard, Jr., Larry, Victor** (pic. August 1967)

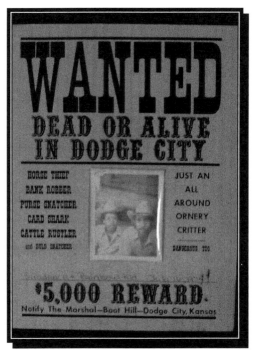

Canard, Jr. and Canard, Sr.
(pic. July 16, 1974)

My Father – *The Rifleman*

Victor Grigsby

My Father – In Florida on "Ringo"

Rev. Canard, Sr., Rev. Victor, and Rev. Canard, Jr.

Canard, Jr., Canard, Sr., and Victor

Victor and Vickie Grigsby

151

Grigsby Family

My Family
Front Row (lr): Tareka, Nerissa, Clarissa, Alonna, Nekesha
Back Row (lr): Brian, Victor, Vickie, Victor, II

ENDNOTES

Chapter 1

[1] According to the A.C. Nielsen Co., the average American watches more than 4 hours of TV each day (or 28 hours/week, or 2 months of nonstop TV-watching per year). In a 65-year life, that person will have spent 9 years glued to the tube.
Percentage of households that possess at least one television: 99
Number of TV sets in the average U.S. household: 2.24
Percentage of U.S. homes with three or more sets: 66
Number of hours per day that TV is on in an average U.S. home:
    6 hours, 47 minutes
Percentage of Americans that regularly watch television while
    eating dinner: 66
Compiled by TV-Free America, 1322 18th Street, NW, Washington, D.C. 20036

[2] Family Reality Television shows like "Run's House," "Family Crews," and "The Osborne's" have become the popular brand of 21st century television.

[3] The Encyclopedia of Childhood and Adolescence, April 6, 2001 defines dysfunctional family as one where the relationships among family members are not conducive to emotional and physical health. Sexual or physical abuse, alcohol and drug addictions, delinquency and behavior problems, eating disorders, and extreme aggression are some conditions commonly associated with dysfunctional family relationships.

Chapter 2

[1] According to the Holy Scriptures, Satan was a spirit in heaven and was the most beautiful and most grand of all the angels. His name was Lucifer, yet when he rebelled in heaven he lost his heavenly estate with God and was banished from the presence of God forever. Isaiah 14:12-15 states, "How art thou fallen, O Lucifer, son of the morning! How art thou cut down to the ground, which didst weaken the nations! For thou hast said in thine heart, I will ascend into the heaven, I will exalt my throne above the stars of God: I will stir also upon the mount of the congregation, in the sides of the north: I will ascend above the heights of the clouds; I will be like the most High. Yet thou shalt be brought down to hell, to the sides of the pit."

[2] Brad Henry, Governor of Oklahoma, State of the State Address, February 7, 2005

[3] St. Augustine of Hippo, *The Trinity*, p.271. An understanding of God the Lover, the Son the beloved, and the Holy Spirit the Love is presented therein.

Chapter 3

[1] These lyrics were from the *Good Times* theme song written by Dave Grusin and Andrew Bergman. *Good Times* is an American sitcom that originally aired from February 8, 1974, until August 1, 1979, on the CBS television network. It was created by Eric Monte and Michael Evans and produced by Norman Lear.

[2] A discussion in Theodicy could be entertained here. Theodicy explores the problem of evil in the world, and raises the question: "Why does an all-good and all-powerful God allow suffering in the world?" One argument is that either God's goodness is flawed, or his power is limited. The term was coined in 1710 by the German philosopher Gottfried Leibniz. The solution to the Theodicy problem is examined by great theologians and philosophers like Richard Swinburne and Christian apologist Gregory A. Boyd.

Chapter 4

[1] Dr. Tessina is a Psychotherapist, self-help author, and licensed Marriage and Family Therapist. She mentions in her book: *It Ends With You: Grow Up and Out of Dysfunction*, February 1, 2002.

[2] Thomas Louis Haines, *The Royal Path of Life,* A. P. T. Elder & Co., Chicago, ILL, 1882.

Chapter 5

[1] George Whitefield mentions in his book, *The Great Duty of Family Religion*, "act in the three capacities that God has required: as a *prophet*, to instruct; as a *priest*, to pray for and with; and as a *king*, to govern, direct, and provide for them, then our families are the strongest and God most pleased

[2] Petersen, J. Allen, *For Men Only,* Living Books Tyndale House Publishers, Inc., Wheaton, Illinois, 1973, P. 56

Chapter 6

[1] At MTV's 1999 Video Music Awards, "Scantily clad Lil' Kim, who was not known as an attention-getter at the time, caused a stir when she walked the red carpet wearing a purple wig and dressed in a purple sequined pantsuit, minus one half of her top. (Well, she WAS modest enough to cover her exposed breast with a matching purple pasty.) Later, when Mary J. Blige and Kim presented an award with [Diana] Ross, Ross opted to greet Kim not by shaking her hand but by jiggling her breast." Also, Super Bowl XXXVIII, which was broadcast live on February 1, 2004 from Houston, Texas on the CBS television network in the United States, was noted for a controversial halftime show in which Janet Jackson's breast, adorned with a nipple shield, was exposed by Justin Timberlake for about half a second, in what was later referred to as a "wardrobe malfunction".

[2] Nelson, Thomas, *The King James Study Bible*, Publishing, Thomas Nelson Publishers, Nashville, TN, 1983, p.11

[3] John Gray, *Men are from Mars, Women are from Venus,* (published in May 1992) is a book that offers many suggestions for improving men-women relationships in couples by understanding the communication style and emotional needs of the opposite gender.

[4] *The Holy Bible, New International Version*, Zondervan Publishing House, Grand Rapids, Michigan, 1984
[5] Tyndale, *Life Application Bible*, Tyndale House Publishers, Inc., Wheaton, Illinois, 1989, p. 2200

[6] *The Holy Bible, Updated New American Standard Bible*, Zondervan Publishing House, Grand Rapids, Michigan, 1999

[7] McRae, William J., *Preparing for Your Marriage*, Zondervan Publishing, Grand Rapids, Michigan, 1980 p. 9

[8] Ibid., p. 9

[9] Ibid., p. 9

[10] Crabb, Larry Dr., *Men & Women: Enjoying The Difference*, Zondervan Publishing House, Grand Rapids, Michigan, 1993, p.199

[11] Ibid., p.199

156

[12] Ibid., p.200

[13] Ibid., p.200

[14] Ibidl, p.200

Chapter 7

[1] Nelson, Thomas, *The King James Study Bible*, Publishing, Thomas Nelson Publishers, Nashville, TN, 1983, p.14

[2] Tyndale, *Life Application Bible,* p.55

[3] The Holy Bible, New International Version

[4] Wikipedia.com: Quality time is an informal reference to time spent with loved ones (*e.g.,* close family, partners or friends) which is in some way important, special, productive or profitable. It is time that is set aside for paying full and undivided attention to the person/matter at hand. It may also refer to time spent performing some favored activity (*e.g.,* a hobby). The opportunity to experience quality time, or the actual time available to enjoy quality time is often limited. However, this is outweighed by the importance, intensity or value attached to events or interactions which occur during quality time. Quality time therefore has a degree of emotional or social "quality" which other aspects of personal life may lack. Busy parents may also use the term to justify the limited amount of overall time they spend with their children

Chapter 8

[1] Dr. Seuss, *Oh, The Places You'll Go*, Random House Publishers, 1990

[2] The Research Network on Transitions to Adulthood by the University of California – Irvine Department of Sociology.
"Those who are no longer attending school may do so subsequently, and those who 'drop out' of college may 'drop in' years after; those who hold a full-time job now may lose it or leave it for any number of reasons. In addition, marriage or cohabitation are scarcely permanent arrangements, but may eventuate in separation or divorce (or in death of a partner) and into a newfound marital status as a single. Even having a child of one's own living in one's household can be subject to status change. Nonetheless, it remains

the case that those traditional normative markers do reflect key exits and entrances into adult status, and as such the typology of the five transitions remains useful as a means to sketch, if with broad brush strokes, a heuristically meaningful empirical portrait of the social situation of young adults." (rrumbaut@uci.edu)

[3] *Reconsider,* a Lifeway Biblical Solutions for Life publication

[4] ibid.

[5] ibid.

[6] www.pregnancy-info.net: In 2000, the total number of teen pregnancies in the United States was 821,810 (84 pregnancies per 1,000 people). Compare this with Canada whose total rate of teen pregnancies for 2000 was 38,600 (38 pregnancies per 1,000 people). In the United States, the 18 - 19 year-old age group has the highest rate of pregnancy followed by the 15 - 17 year-old age group. However, 15 – 17 year-old pregnancy rates dropped by as much as 23% between 1992 and 2000, while the rate for 18 to 19 year-olds only dropped by 11%.
-Nationally, nearly one million young women under age 20 become pregnant each year. That means close to 2800 teens get pregnant each day.(Facts in Brief: Teen Sex and Pregnancy, The Alan Guttmacher Institute, New York, 1996).

-Approximately 4 in 10 young women in the U.S. become pregnant at least once before turning 20 years old.(Facts in Brief: Teen Sex and Pregnancy, The Alan Guttmacher Institute, New York, 1996).

-Teen childbearing alone costs U.S. taxpayers nearly $7 billion annually for social services and lost tax revenues. (Kids Having Kids: Economic Costs and Social Consequences of Teen Pregnancy, Prebecca Maynard (ed.), The Urban Institute, Washington, DC, 1997).

Chapter 9

[1] Bacon, Francis, *Apothegm*

[2] Edward F. Markquart, *Aging and All Saints*, Sermons from Seattle, info@sfs.com. "The agrarian society of 3400 years ago and our present society have similar outlooks concerning the working man and woman: not much has changed – their value is severely reduced at about age sixty."

[3] *The World Health Organization* Copyright © 2000-2010 NHIOnDemand, LLC All rights reserved.

www.nhiondemand.com. "In 2000 there were 600 million people aged sixty and over; there will be 1.2 billion by 2025, and 2 billion by 2050. In the developed world, the very old (age 80+) is the fastest growing population group."

[4] Edward F. Markquart, *Aging and All Saints*, Sermons from Seattle, info@sfs.com.

[5] Morgan, Robert J., *Nelson's Complete Book Of: Stories, Illustrations & Quotes,* Thomas Nelson Publishing, Nashville, TN., p. 15

Chapter 10

[1] Tyndale, *Life Application Bible*, p. 1587

[2] Nelson, Thomas, *The King James Study Bible*, Publishing, Thomas Nelson Publishers, Nashville, TN, 1983, p. 1439

[3] Tyndale, *Life Application Bible*, p. 1965

[4] Ibib., p. 2073

[5] Ibid., p.207

[6] Tyndale, *Life Application Bible*, p. 1733

[7] Ibid., p. 1093

/